LAW SCHOOL SURVIVAL MANUAL

ASPEN PUBLISHERS

LAW SCHOOL SURVIVAL MANUAL: FROM LSAT TO BAR EXAM

Nancy B. Rapoport and Jeffrey D. Van Niel

Wolters Kluwer
Law & Business

AUSTIN   BOSTON   CHICAGO   NEW YORK   THE NETHERLANDS

Aspen Publishers
Attn: Permissions Department
76 Ninth Avenue, 7th Floor
New York, NY 10011-5201

To contact Customer Care, e-mail customer.service@aspenpublishers.com, call 1-800-234-1660, fax 1-800-901-9075, or mail correspondence to:

Aspen Publishers
Attn: Order Department
PO Box 990
Frederick, MD 21705

Printed in the United States of America.

1 2 3 4 5 6 7 8 9 0

ISBN 978-0-7355-9490-6

Library of Congress Cataloging-in-Publication Data

Rapoport, Nancy B.
    Law school survival manual : from LSAT to bar exam / Nancy B. Rapoport, Jeffrey D. Van Niel.
        p. cm.
    Includes index.
    ISBN 978-0-7355-9490-6 (pbk. : alk. paper)   1. Law-Study and teaching-United States. 2. Law students-United States-Handbooks, manuals, etc. I. Van Niel, Jeffrey D. II. Title.
    KF283.R37 2010
    340.071'173-dc22

                                                                    2010015684

About Wolters Kluwer Law & Business

Wolters Kluwer Law & Business is a leading provider of research information and workflow solutions in key specialty areas. The strengths of the individual brands of Aspen Publishers, CCH, Kluwer Law International and Loislaw are aligned within Wolters Kluwer Law & Business to provide comprehensive, in-depth solutions and expert-authored content for the legal, professional and education markets.

CCH was founded in 1913 and has served more than four generations of business professionals and their clients. The CCH products in the Wolters Kluwer Law & Business group are highly regarded electronic and print resources for legal, securities, antitrust and trade regulation, government contracting, banking, pension, payroll, employment and labor, and healthcare reimbursement and compliance professionals.

Aspen Publishers is a leading information provider for attorneys, business professionals and law students. Written by preeminent authorities, Aspen products offer analytical and practical information in a range of specialty practice areas from securities law and intellectual property to mergers and acquisitions and pension/benefits. Aspen's trusted legal education resources provide professors and students with high-quality, up-to-date and effective resources for successful instruction and study in all areas of the law.

Kluwer Law International supplies the global business community with comprehensive English-language international legal information. Legal practitioners, corporate counsel and business executives around the world rely on the Kluwer Law International journals, loose-leafs, books and electronic products for authoritative information in many areas of international legal practice.

Loislaw is a premier provider of digitized legal content to small law firm practitioners of various specializations. Loislaw provides attorneys with the ability to quickly and efficiently find the necessary legal information they need, when and where they need it, by facilitating access to primary law as well as state-specific law, records, forms and treatises.

Wolters Kluwer Law & Business, a unit of Wolters Kluwer, is headquartered in New York and Riverwoods, Illinois. Wolters Kluwer is a leading multinational publisher and information services company.

CONTENTS

ABOUT THE AUTHORS

Nancy B. Rapoport is the Gordon Silver Professor at the William S. Boyd School of Law, University of Nevada, Las Vegas. After receiving her BA, summa cum laude, from Rice University in 1982 and her JD from Stanford Law School in 1985, she clerked for the Honorable Joseph T. Sneed on the U.S. Court of Appeals for the Ninth Circuit and then practiced law (primarily bankruptcy law) with Morrison & Foerster in San Francisco from 1986 to 1991. She started her academic career at The[1] Ohio State University College of Law in 1991, and she moved from Assistant Professor to Associate Professor with tenure (1995) to Associate Dean for Student Affairs (1996) and Professor in 1998 (just as she left Ohio State to become Dean and Professor of Law at the University of Nebraska College of Law). She served as Dean of the University of Nebraska College of Law from 1998 to 2000. She then served as Dean and Professor of Law at the University of Houston Law Center from July 2000 until May 2006 and as Professor of Law from June 2006 until June 2007, when she left to join the faculty at Boyd.

Her specialties are bankruptcy ethics, ethics in governance, and the depiction of lawyers in popular culture. Among her published works is *Enron: Corporate Fiascos and Their Implications* (Foundation Press 2004, co-edited with Professor Bala G. Dharan of Rice University), for which Jeffrey D. Van Niel was a stealth co-editor. The second edition, *Enron and Other Corporate Fiascos: The Corporate Scandal Reader* (Nancy B. Rapoport, Jeffrey D. Van Niel, and Bala G. Dharan, eds., Foundation Press 2d ed., 2009), addresses the question of why people never seem to learn from prior corporate scandals. She is admitted to the bars of the states of California, Ohio,

---

[1] "The" really *is* capitalized as part of The Ohio State University's official name.

Nebraska, Texas, and Nevada and of the U.S. Supreme Court. In 2001, she was elected to membership in the American Law Institute, and in 2002, she received a Distinguished Alumna Award from Rice University. She is a Fellow of the American Bar Foundation and a Fellow of the American College of Bankruptcy. In 2009, the Association of Media and Entertainment Counsel presented her with the Public Service Counsel Award at the 4th Annual Counsel of the Year Awards.

She has also appeared as herself in the Academy Award®–nominated movie, *Enron: The Smartest Guys in the Room* (Magnolia Pictures 2005). Although the movie garnered her a listing at *www.imdb.com*, she still hasn't been able to join the Screen Actors Guild. In her spare time, she competes, pro-am, in ballroom and Latin dance with her teacher, Sergei Shapoval.

Jeffrey D. Van Niel is a native of Columbus, Ohio. He enlisted in the U.S. Marine Corps immediately after graduating from high school in 1976. After four years of service in the Marines as a scout sniper and remote sensor operator, he received an Honorable Discharge and joined the Ohio State Highway Patrol. He left the Highway Patrol in 1981 to get a bachelor's degree in criminal justice at Ohio University in 1983. He started law school in 1984 in lieu of joining the Secret Service (and never looked back). Mr. Van Niel served as Executive Notes Editor for the Capital University Law Review, and he received his JD from Capital University Law School in 1987, cum laude, having received the honors of the Order of the Curia and the Order of the Barristers. He clerked for Ohio Supreme Court Justice Andrew Douglas after graduation, and in 1988, he joined the Cleveland law firm of Hahn Loeser ▲ Parks.[2] When one of the firm's partners became the Ohio Attorney General and another partner became the chairman of the Ohio Public Utilities Commission, Mr. Van Niel followed them to serve in the Ohio Attorney General's Public Utilities Commission Practice Group. He volunteered for a second tour of duty with the Supreme Court of Ohio in 1993 as the Court's Utilities Law Master Commissioner. Moving from Ohio to Nebraska to Houston (to join his wife every time that she changed academic positions), Mr. Van Niel worked as

---

[2] The ▲ is really in Hahn Loeser's firm name, too.

a consultant until 2004, when he joined the Harris County Community Service and Corrections Department as Staff Counsel. In yet another move to satisfy his wife's wanderlust, this time to Las Vegas, Mr. Van Niel became a consultant in regulatory and governmental affairs to Nye County in the Yucca Mountain licensing proceeding in October 2007. He is admitted to the bars of the states of Ohio, Nebraska, Texas, and Nevada, and he served as a former bar examiner in Ohio. He is also the primary caregiver to the couple's two cats, Shadow and Grace.

Introduction

When we first thought about writing this book, we were skeptical. With all of the "how to survive law school" books out there already, was there really anything new to say? But when we looked at the other books—many of which are very good—we noticed a couple of things missing. First, most of the other books take you from the application process through the first year of law school. That's fine, as far as it goes, but you need to know about the rest of law school if you're really going to survive the process. Second, none of the other books is written from the viewpoint of two people who had entirely different experiences in law school. One of us (Jeff) went to law school while working full-time; the other one (Nancy) had the luxury of parents who were paying for law school. One of us (again, Jeff) went to a school that focused on practical lawyering; the other one (you guessed it: Nancy) went to a school that assumed that students would learn how to be a lawyer after graduation. (We'd also point out that one of us paid more attention to the material he learned in law school than the other one did, but that would not be helpful during our family reunions. After all, we're married, and our in-laws know each other.) Our experiences after law school have been similar: clerking for a judge, then big-firm practice, then leaving big-firm life to follow our passions. If nothing else, the fact that our postgraduation experiences were similar is proof positive that, even though where you go to law school is important, what you do while you are there (and what you do afterward) will be more important.

Our book is also different because it really is a survival manual. It's not going to take you through all the various parts of the law school experience; rather, it focuses on the parts that we think need extra survival skills. We've divided the book into segments that actually occur in real life, and we'll give you tools for dealing with each of those segments. One of us has used real survival manuals before, in his life as a Marine. The other one wishes that she'd had a survival manual in law school, because she knows that she would have gotten much more out of the experience if she'd been better prepared.

You might want to reread various chapters of this manual from time to time. For one thing, like many aspects of law school, some knowledge takes a while to sink in. Repetition might help. Moreover, if you've made it through some of the tougher stages of law school, you might get some comfort from seeing how far you've come from those first few days of extreme uncertainty and confusion.

You'll find that we both write in an informal tone of voice, and that we share the same sardonic sense of humor. Although we're both lawyers, and we know how to write in a formal tone of voice when it's appropriate to do so, we're writing to you as if we were having a series of conversations over coffee. We don't want to scare you. We just want you to survive this odd process called law school.

Although we come at this manual from different perspectives, we agree on one critical issue. Our philosophy is simple: In some ways, law school is like war. You're at war with your old habits; you're at war with the material. One thing to remember, though: You're *not* at war with your classmates, even if your school has a mandatory grading curve. Your classmates are on *your* team and, although you might be sorely tempted from time to time, friendly fire is not allowed.

Life is full of obstacles; you need to overcome them. Planning your mission is critical to success. We think that this book will help.

Acknowledgments

We could not have written this book without the hard work of many people, including Nettie Mann, the good folks at Aspen (especially Steve Errick, Lynn Churchill, Carol McGeehan, Carmen Corral-Reid, and Jessica Barmack), and those patient people who read earlier drafts and gave us all sorts of help and encouragement: Rachel Anderson, Cynthia Asher, Mark Bell, Whitney Blair (who helped us come up with the subtitle of the book), Carol Brown, Jennifer Carr, Frank Durand, Linda Edwards, Rodney Fong, Adrienne Gasser, Catherine Glaze, Jennifer Gross, Kirk Homeyer, Hank and Demaris Hudspeth, Amee McKim (who gave us great suggestions and an amazing line-by-line edit), and Morris Rapoport. I want to thank my beloved husband, Jeff Van Niel, who sat next to me, typing on his laptop, as we traded drafts back and forth, as well as my wonderful parents, Morris and Shirley Rapoport, whose hard work raising me and putting me through college and law school set me on the world's best career path. Finally, I want to thank all of my students over the years, who have made teaching such a joy. In particular (and not to slight any of the others), I want to remember Robert Allen, whose passing was all too soon and whose joy in learning the law was infectious. For Robert, a fedora salute:

—Nancy

I want to thank Nancy Rapoport, my loving wife, who worked extremely hard and allowed us to meet our deadline for this book. I'm sure that the cattle prod did not leave permanent marks. Without her, this book would have remained just a series of bland discussions between two attorneys.

—Jeff

CHAPTER ONE

Before Law School Begins

Strength does not come from physical capacity. It comes from an indomitable will.

— **Mohandas K. Gandhi**

1. The Basics: What You'll Need Before You Apply for Admission to Law School

So you want to go to law school. Great! We're glad that you're interested. There are a lot of good reasons to choose a legal education. You might want to become a lawyer (most people who go to law school do), or you might just want to understand how the legal system works. But there are a few things that you need to ask yourself before you begin the process.

1. *Do you like to read?* No matter which law school you attend, law school involves an exorbitant amount of reading. If reading is not one of your favorite things to do—or, at the very least, if you don't have a high tolerance for reading mass quantities of material—you might want to put our book down and back slowly away.

2. *Are you good at studying?* If your undergraduate career involved spending countless hours working by yourself to master various subjects, then you're probably prepared to enter law school. If, on the other hand, you breezed through college without cracking many books open and got by with cramming for finals at the last second, then you're likely going to have to revamp your study skills. Law school is more "tortoise" than "hare."

3. *Are you comfortable with your writing ability?* Many undergraduate majors don't require a lot of writing; others require very specific types of writing, like scientific reports. Law school—especially your first year—involves writing a

lot of papers and honing your analytical and persuasive skills. If you freeze up when someone asks you to write a paper, you need to think hard about your potential career choice. Lawyers write something almost every day.

4. *Do you know what lawyers do?* Okay, this one's a trick question. Jeff knew what some lawyers did before he thought about entering law school. He watched them appear in court to testify, and he thought to himself, "I can do what these folks are doing." Nancy, on the other hand, had no idea what lawyers did when she was deciding what to do after college. All she knew is that lawyers didn't have to deal with a lot of blood and that law seemed to be more of an indoor job than an outdoor one. For her, those reasons worked. It's totally fine if you have no idea what lawyers do, as long as you know that you like to read, you can buckle down and study, and you can express ideas in writing. Lawyers can do all sorts of things. They don't all appear in court. Heck, they don't all practice law: Some lawyers run companies. But—and we're serious about this point—all lawyers do three things: They think, they read, and they write. If you enjoy those things, you're on the right track.

There are a million good reasons to go to law school, but there are also some bad reasons. Don't go to law school expecting to get rich. Most lawyers earn a comfortable living, but only a small percentage of them will earn enough to get rich. Choosing a career solely because of its earning capacity can set you up for misery. If you don't like what you do, every day's work will be a chore. If you enjoy what you do, that job satisfaction goes a long way.

We're also not fans of the idea that you should go to law school because that's what people in your family "do" or because your family thinks that you would make a good lawyer. Your family isn't going to do the day-to-day work of your legal career; you are. Make a decision based on what career makes the most sense for you.

But for those of you who are going to law school because you don't have any idea what you want to do in life, we think that reason's not so bad at all. Law school is like the last grand liberal arts education. You'll get exposed to new ways of thinking about complex problems. You'll examine policies for organizing human behavior. You'll learn the difference between making arguments based on emotion and arguments based on reason. All in all, law school is a great way to expand your view of how the world works.

Ready to get started? Good. Before you can apply to an ABA[1]-accredited law school,[2] you're going to need an undergraduate degree and an LSAT score.

1.1. The LSAT

The Law School Admission Council (LSAC) administers the Law School Admission Test (LSAT).[3] The idea behind the LSAT is that law school admissions committees would find it useful, in addition to reviewing applicants' individual backgrounds, to compare applicants based on their scores on a standardized test. The LSAC's Web site, *http://www.lsac.org*, provides plenty of information on the LSAT itself, so we won't rehash that information here. Instead, we just want to give you some thoughts about how to approach the LSAT.

If you're good at taking multiple-choice tests, you're in luck. The scored portion of the LSAT consists of five[4] sections of multiple-choice questions, plus an unscored writing section. If you're not good at taking multiple-choice tests, then you should come up with a plan to practice taking the LSAT. The LSAC itself has some study aids that you can order. You can, of course, also take a prep course, although they're pretty expensive. The LSAT is a high-stakes test, so it's worth taking the time to practice the skills that you'll need.

Let's say that you sit for the LSAT, and you're not happy with your score. First, you need to remember that the actual LSAT score

---

[1] ABA stands for American Bar Association, the group that accredits law schools (among other things). *See http://www.abanet.org/legaled/*.

[2] And you really should limit your search to ABA-accredited law schools, if at all possible (including those that are just getting started and are provisionally accredited). Getting a degree from a school that is merely state-accredited and not ABA-accredited could limit your ability to sit for the bar exam in a different state from the one in which that school is located.

[3] *http://www.lsac.org/*.

[4] Actually, four out of the five sections are scored. One of the five is an unscored, experimental section designed to test new questions.

represents a band of scores: For example, a score of 150 actually means that, on any given day, your score for that administration of that test could be anything from 147 to 153. We know that this information isn't particularly reassuring for you, but that band-score concept matters. Before you rush off and register to take the test again, you need to ask yourself why you were disappointed in your score. Did you prepare for the LSAT before you took it? If not, then maybe you should spend more time studying, and perhaps you should take the test again. Be aware, though, that some law schools will average your two LSAT scores when they review your file, others will look at the trend of your multiple scores, and still others will focus on your most recent or highest scores. Were you feeling ill when you took the test? (Nancy got hives the night before the LSAT that were so bad that her parents rushed her to the emergency room.) Was something going on nearby that distracted you? (Jeff took the test while a marching band contest was occurring right outside the test center.) If you think that the reason that your LSAT score was disappointing was due to a one-shot problem, then you should consider retaking the exam.

If, however, you studied for the LSAT, and you didn't have a marching band practicing outside the test center or come down with a bad cold the day before, then perhaps you should just accept your score for what it is: one number (albeit an important one) that's part of your admissions file. Schools look at more than just your LSAT score when they review your admissions file. They'll look at your undergraduate grade-point average (GPA), any additional degrees that you might have earned, your personal statement, your resume, your letters of recommendation, and any other information that they deem relevant. So let's make sure that the rest of your file is as good as it can be.

1.2. Your Grades

Most law schools put applicants' files into the virtual equivalent of three piles: "automatically admit," "automatically deny," and "think about these files some more." The "automatic" piles aren't really automatic, but they're there to winnow down the hundreds or thousands of applications that each law school gets. You'll be in the "automatically admit" pile if your LSAT score and your undergraduate GPA hit the mysterious secret threshold for that school.[5] If you're in that pile, the school will admit you unless there's something else in your file (say, a conviction for murder)[6] that might give the school some pause.

If your LSAT score and GPA are far lower than those of any of the school's successful students, you're likely going to be in the "automatically deny" pile. Factors that can pull you out of that pile can include a high LSAT score but a low GPA (or vice versa); significant improvement in your GPA during the course of your undergraduate career; a valid explanation for a bad GPA or LSAT score;[7] an advanced degree, with a high GPA, that you earned long after your college degree; or a really compelling personal statement.

Most applicants' files fall into that large middle "let's think about these files some more" pile. If your LSAT score and GPA are average for that school—or slightly above or below average—you're likely going to be in that middle pile. Moving from that pile into the admit pile will depend on a variety of factors, some of which are within your control and some of which aren't. You can control how compelling your personal statement is and how well-written it is in general; you can't control how your statement compares to the statements of the other applicants in your application cycle. You can control whom you choose to write letters of recommendation; you can't control what they say about you. You have some control over your GPA while you're earning it, but once you've gotten your degree, your GPA is just a fact—no longer within your control. Like your LSAT score, once you've earned

---

[5] For you statistics geeks out there, Nancy wants you to know that what actually happens is that each school uses a multivariate regression analysis that calculates beta coefficients for the LSAT scores and the undergraduate GPA scores so that the school can relate applicants' LSATs and GPAs to their predicted first-year grades at that school. The LSAC can calibrate these multipliers for the school, or the school can come up with its own weights for the LSAT and GPA.

[6] If you *are* a convicted murderer, you should know that at least one law school has admitted a convicted murderer. *See http://www.cbsnews.com/stories/2004/10/13/60II/main649084.shtml.*

[7] Valid explanations for a bad GPA can include serious illness or caregiving responsibilities while in school. Valid explanations for a low LSAT score can include the unusual situations that we described in Section 1.1 as well as a demonstration that your undergraduate standardized test score underpredicted your undergraduate GPA.

your GPA, it's just another part of your application file. If it's strong, that's great; if it's not so strong, you need to ask yourself what you can offer to those schools to which you're applying that other applicants might not be able to offer. In other words, what can *you* add to an entering class? And guess what? You'll be able to tell the schools just what you can offer with a well-written personal statement.

1.3.   Your Personal Statement

Writing your personal statement is by far the most difficult part of the law school application process. We know that you'll spend hours staring at a blank piece of paper or a blank document on your computer screen trying to figure out what to say. The good news is that there's no one good way to write a personal statement; there are infinite good ways. Of course, the bad news is that we still haven't told you what to write.

We can't tell you what to write, but we can tell you what you're trying to achieve: You're trying to tell the admissions committee what you bring to the table. You're also showing the admissions committee how well you (and your family and friends, who have edited your statement) can write. You can talk about why you want to be a lawyer, or about why you think you'd add to the law school community. You can talk about your family background or about the democratic process and its effect on public policy. There's no one right subject. Just make sure that your paragraphs make sense and flow easily together and that you've caught any errors in grammar and spelling. And, in the long run, you'll have to ask yourself what we have had to ask ourselves as we wrote this book: Does each paragraph that you've written make someone want to keep reading?

1.4.   Getting the Most Useful Letters of Recommendation

Forget the letters from famous or well-connected people who barely know you. Those letters really don't help your application file at all, because they don't tell the admissions committee what it needs to know: What will you be like as a law student? Admissions committees want letters of recommendation to address what the recommender knows about you, based on personal experience. Will you participate actively in class? Are you likely to thrive in the law school environment? Might your life experiences add to class discussions or to your future classmates' discussions outside of the classroom? Do you write well? Do you have a sense of humor?

Find people who know you well enough to answer those questions for the admissions committee. It doesn't matter if those people are professors who are extremely well known or graduate students who are just starting their careers. What matters is how well they know you.

Think of your application file as a puzzle. You have pieces of that puzzle—your resume, the answers to the questions on the school's application, your personal statement, your LSAT score, your undergraduate GPA, and your letters of recommendation— and each of those pieces, standing alone, shows only a part of who you are and what you can do. You can't afford to have one of those pieces (the letters of recommendation) rehash the other pieces without adding some new information. Each of those pieces needs to build your case.

1.5. Other Admissions Issues

Not everyone comes to law school with a stellar record. We've often said that we're surprised that people survive into adulthood, given how many dumb mistakes we all make growing up. If some of your dumb mistakes have made their way into a file about you, such as a police file, all isn't lost. But you do have to acknowledge in your application any of those public-record mistakes and explain them. Don't assume that your failure to mention them will keep law schools from finding out about them. (Don't even assume that expunged records are safe from discovery, unless you're holding an expungement order in your hands.)

In law, as in life, the best practice is to disclose information and explain it, rather than hide it with the hope that that information will never come to light. Not only can a law school revoke your admission if it finds out that you've been hiding something important, but the failure to mention those important public-record issues on your law school application can actually hold up your

Yet another way to look for schools in your specialty is to check the specialty listings in *U.S. News & World Report* or similar rankings. Although we're both extremely skeptical about the validity of the general *U.S. News & World Report* rankings (as we discuss in Section 2.5, below), at least the specialty rankings consist of votes of some of the faculty members in that specialty. There might still be ways to game the system—do you really think that school 5 on a specialty list is going to rank schools 1 through 4 highly?—but overall, the specialty rankings are a reasonable way of double-checking your own research.

What if you really, really want to do public interest law when you graduate? (Public interest law helps underserved communities or poor people.) These types of jobs are wonderful, but they don't pay very well. We strongly recommend that you choose a school that minimizes your debt load. Generally speaking, when you take out student loans, you must pay them back—virtually all student loans are not dischargeable in bankruptcy cases. Even if you're math-phobic, consider this point: If you take out $100,000 in law school loans, you will have to pay back $100,000 in law school loans, plus interest. If you're making less than $30,000 a year in a public interest job, you will not be able to simultaneously pay back your loans, eat, and pay rent or a mortgage. The arithmetic just doesn't crunch in your favor. So instead of incurring that massive debt and then finding yourself in a huge financial crisis, do your math ahead of time. Choose a school that you can afford. (We'll talk more about loans—and about managing your loans and public interest work—in Chapter 2. In the meantime, the good news is that many schools have loan repayment assistance programs (LRAPs). For the Federal LRAP, created by the College Cost Reduction and Access Act of 2007, *see http://www.abanet.org/legalservices/sclaid/lrap/federallrap.html*. LRAPs enable some students to manage their law school debt while working in the public interest.)

2.2.   *Choosing a Law School When You Want to Keep Your Options Open*

If you have no idea what you want to do after law school (and most law students don't), then your choice will probably depend on some combination of the following factors: (1) how well you did in your undergraduate career; (2) how high you scored on your LSAT; (3) what other sorts of "plusses" you bring to the table when you're being considered for admission; (4) how much "law school" you can afford; and (5) how important a good network (supportive administrators and professors, along with an active alumni association) is to you.

Let's look at the best case scenario first. If you had a stellar undergraduate GPA at an intellectually challenging undergraduate institution and you get a perfect (or almost perfect) LSAT score, congratulations! You'll be in the ballpark for some very impressive schools. Some of those schools might even offer you a scholarship. If you're in this happy group, try to visit the schools with the best reputations. Don't just look at *U.S. News & World Report.* Professor Brian Leiter has a law school ranking system (*http://www. leiterrankings.com/*) that is based on the scholarly reputation of the schools' faculty members—the people who will be teaching you while you're in school there. Other rankings systems include Professor Kristen Crawford's rankings based on the number of downloads of law professor articles posted on the Social Science Research Network (*http://feministlawprofessors.com/?p=11712*) and Professor Jeffrey Stake's "Law School Rankings Game" (*http:// monoborg.law.indiana.edu/LawRank/*). Look at all of the rankings, and try to visit as many schools as you can. (Some schools, if they really want you, will even pay for you to travel to visit them.[8]) If you can visit the school while classes are in session, so much the better. Sit in on some classes, and talk to some of the students afterward. Are the students friendly? Do they introduce themselves to you after class? Do you feel as if you fit in at the school? Do the students seem as if they like each other? Do they socialize in the hallways?

See where you feel most comfortable—where the school fits your personality. If you're looking at the schools at the very top of the pecking order, you can't go wrong, so go with your gut about where you'd be happiest. The best thing about going to one of these top schools is that your classmates (and your professors) will be national and international movers and shakers. In other words, if you don't become an absolute jerk during law school, you will

---

[8] If you are—as we were—not a member of that elite group, please don't feel intimidated or otherwise miffed. Neither of us was chosen to play professional sports, either, and we've survived quite well anyway.

likely have the ability, for the rest of your professional career, to have access to some pretty powerful people. By the way, if you have the ability to get into a top-notch state (flagship) law school, that school will have many of the same networking advantages—at least at the state or regional level.

If you don't fall into the best-case scenario (very few do, so don't fret), you have some more legwork to do. You won't get the red-carpet treatment, although most schools have very good admissions officers who will be happy to give you a tour of the school and let you sit in on some classes. Although you should have some feel about picking a school based on your under-graduate experience, we recommend that you visit some law schools, if you can afford the time and expense, so that you can get a sense of whether you prefer a large or small school (with lots of small sections or lots of large classes), in a rural or urban setting. You might also want to think about whether you prefer a private or public law school, although the tuition differentials between public and private law schools are starting to shrink.

In any event, you *need* to pay attention to the following considerations:

1.   What is the school's first-time pass rate for the bar, and how does that pass rate compare to the state's overall bar pass rate?[9]

2.   How does the school's career services department help stu-dents find jobs? How many students have law-related jobs at graduation? Nine months after? (Don't be fooled by the *U.S. News & World Report* "placement" statistics: As of the time that we wrote this book, "placement" includes any job, not just a law-related job.)

3.   What kind of academic support program does the school have?

---

[9] For example, we've both taken the Nevada Bar (among other bar exams). That bar has an extremely low pass rate. When Nancy took the bar, the pass rate was 66 percent; when Jeff took it, the pass rate was around 55 percent. Compared to the state's overall pass rate, then, the pass rate at the William S. Boyd School of Law, UNLV, of over 85 percent looks pretty good, doesn't it?

4. How accessible are the professors? Do they keep regular office hours?

5. How friendly and helpful are the students? Are they supportive of each other, or do they tend to be cutthroat?[10]

6. How many students are dismissed for academic problems each year?

If you can schedule a time to meet with the career services dean,[11] with some professors, and with the dean of students or academic support dean, so much the better. If they're not responsive to you while you're deciding among schools (we like to call this phase the "dating" phase), how responsive are they likely to be once you've signed on the dotted line and rejected all of the other possible schools that you could have attended (the "relationship" phase)?

If you can get information on the following questions, so much the better:

1. How active are the alumni in the day-to-day life of the school? Do they mentor current students? (Will you be able to get their advice about jobs—or possibly get jobs from them?) Do they serve on the boards of student organizations? What percentage of the alumni contributes to the school? Do they teach as adjuncts (or better yet, as tenured or tenure-track professors)?

2. Do students live on campus? Near campus? How expensive is it to live in that geographic area? Will you need a car to get around?

---

[10] Ask the school to give you the contact information of some students who will answer your questions about student life—and professor accessibility—at the school. These students will all be wildly biased in favor of that school, because no school is going to give you the contact information for disgruntled students. But if you understand the context of the information that you're getting, the information should be useful.

[11] Warning: The career services dean might be far too busy to talk with you personally before you've entered law school. That dean is helping the already enrolled students with their job searches. But if you happen to have an opportunity to talk with this dean, or one of the other professionals in that department, you could get some very useful information.

3. Do people seem happy there? Do they seem to like the school? Are they proud to be there?

Again, we want to remind you that you're not a one-size-fits-all person. Do some research, and try to find a school that suits *you*. You will likely be considerably happier if you choose a school that fits you, rather than simply walking in cold on the first day of orientation with no information.

2.3. Choosing a Law School When You Have Geographic Restrictions

Let's assume that you need to stay in a particular geographical location for a while. Perhaps you have caregiving responsibilities for some loved ones; maybe your own job (or a loved one's job) prevents you from leaving a certain area. Maybe you need to go to law school on a part-time basis. All of these reasons will move you toward the law school (or law schools) in a particular area.[12] (If you live and need to stay in Alaska, you're going to have a problem. Alaska doesn't have a law school anywhere in the state.)

The good news is that part of your decision has been made for you. The better news is that, if there is more than one school in your area, you should be able to visit all of them, which will let you test the "fit" of each school. You still should try to get answers to the questions posed earlier, but being on site at each school will help you with that intangible "this feels right" or "this feels wrong" part of choosing a school.

Still can't decide? Then go back to a school's reputation. How well regarded is that school in the geographic area in which it's located? Regionally? Nationally? How is it regarded in the area in which you're going to be living after you graduate? Ask around. Sometimes, you'll be surprised by what "people" think of a particular school. And by "people," we mean lawyers and

---

[12] If you can't relocate and your area has only one school, then you know exactly where you are going to go to school. Even if this school is not your first choice, relax—you're still going to law school! Life is full of compromises. Attending a school other than your first choice school does not mean that your career will be derailed.

judges. Those are the people who might be hiring you after you graduate.

2.4. Choosing a Law School When You Have No Idea Why You Want to Go to Law School

One of us went to law school because she didn't want to be a doctor or an engineer. One of us went to law school because he saw lawyers in court and figured out, fairly quickly, that he could do a better job than most of them were doing. (And, by the way, he was correct.) There is nothing wrong with going to law school because you don't want to get an advanced degree in anything else.[13] But for your own sanity, *please* make sure that you actually enjoy reading large batches of material, because you will be reading tens (sometimes hundreds) of pages a day for three years (four, if you go part-time). *Please* make sure that you care enough about detail work to worry about such matters as whether sea lions or seals have external ears, because sometimes a case will turn on such a matter. *Please* make sure that you have the discipline to stay on top of the workload, because—and one of us didn't know this until long after she graduated—you really do need to know all of what you're learning in law school to be a good lawyer. And *please* make sure that you pay attention to how much law school will cost. Law schools can cost upwards of $100,000, and that debt is not likely to be discharged in a bankruptcy. Law school can be a very expensive mistake if you find out that you really don't like this type of education.

Good law students, like good lawyers, work hard. Hard work is part of being a lawyer—or being any type of professional, for that matter. If you are not currently a hard worker, can you buckle down and do the work when it is necessary? If you're not a hard worker, please consider doing something else besides law school. Don't cheat when you ask yourself this question; cheating is guaranteed to do long-term career damage. Really search your soul to figure out if you have the ability to work more than a ten-hour

---

[13] As a way of figuring out if you want to be a lawyer, you might want to read some books about lawyers—fictional and real—who led inspirational lives. We provide a partial list in Section 3 and in Chapter 2.

in criminal law and evidence. Although you might not need any background reading, you might feel more comfortable if you take a look at the following books:

- Grant Gilmore, *The Ages of American Law* (1979) (a short history of various legal philosophy movements).
- Grant Gilmore, *The Death of Contract* (2d ed., 1995) (a short study of how contract law has changed over the years).
- Richard A. Posner, *Economic Analysis of Law* (7th ed., 2007) (the classic text on balancing competing considerations in law).

At the other end of the spectrum, away from intellectually preparing you for studying law, are books that tell you how bizarre law school can be:

- Martha Kimes, *Ivy Briefs: True Tales of a Neurotic Law Student* (2008).
- Lawrence Dieker, Jr., *Letters from Law School: The Life of a Second-Year Law Student* (2000).
- John Jay Osborne, Jr., *The Paper Chase* (2003).
- Scott Turow, *One L: The Turbulent True Story of a First Year at Harvard Law School* (1997).

The third and fourth books on this list scared the heck out of one of us (she read earlier editions of these two books), and the other one, quite sensibly, never read them. All of the books on this second list are about particular people, who experienced particular law schools at particular times in those schools' histories. Read them if you like, because they'll give you a feel for how much pressure law students tend to put on themselves, but don't take them as a forecast of how you'll feel during law school.

One of Nancy's colleagues, Professor Linda Edwards, had a suggestion that had nothing to do with books about law or law school but will help you if you're not used to doing very detailed readings of texts: You might try reading some fiction and then read someone's analysis of that fiction, or reading some poetry and then read someone's exposition of that poem. By observing how someone else parses a word, sentence, or paragraph to derive meaning from it, you can practice the skill that you'll need as you start to read cases and statutes.[14]

4.   Know Yourself

Before we can give you some survival strategies for law school, we need for you to spend a little time thinking about yourself: how you handle stress and how you learn best. Then, when you read the rest of this book, you can apply our advice in a way that best suits you.

4.1.   The Typical Law Student Personality

There are all sorts of law students and law student "personality" studies, and nothing we say here should make you nervous if you don't find yourself fitting into the "typical law student" mold. But there are some attributes that people have found in many law students (even though both of us don't have all of these attributes—and any particular law student might not have many of them):[15]

- Competitive (but not necessarily a nasty style of competitiveness);
- Assertive;
- Confident (but see our discussion of the "impostor syndrome" below);
- Dominant;
- Leadership-oriented;
- Socially comfortable;
- Extroverted; and
- Achievement-oriented.[16]

---

[14] You can, of course, also look at books that talk about these skills in their direct application to law school, but you might want to wait to see which books your legal writing professor assigns to your class.

[15] For a good review of these studies, *see* Susan Daicoff, *Lawyer, Know Thyself: A Review of Empirical Research on Attorney Attributes Bearing on Professionalism,* 46 Am. U. L. Rev. 1337 (1997).

[16] *See id.* at 1362-1385.

Sounds like a pretty successful set of attributes, right? Now imagine that you're standing in a room with 300 to 500 people, and that 90 percent of that room is filled with people with the same set of attributes. That's a lot of alpha people in one room. Now you're getting a feel for what orientation at law school will be like.

Here's another way to think of typical law student personalities. Most personality attributes are randomly distributed, so that, in any given group of people, the distribution, say, of talent might have a standard bell curve distribution. In that distribution, you're likely going to fall with the overachievers at the far right end of the curve.

Don't get too excited. Every specialty has the same characteristic: Elite athletes have their own "you are here" area on a bell curve, too; so do champion cup-stackers.

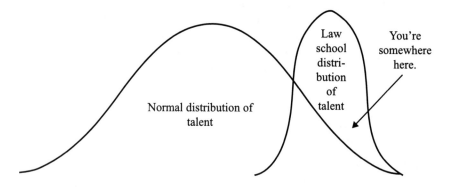

What do these graphics mean? There will be a lot of people just like you in law school. You've all been stars, and now virtually all of you will be in the middle of the pack—but you're in a "pack" that is made up of really, really smart people. That's good (mostly), but occasionally a bit oppressive. Just be prepared.

One more note: Really successful people often experience something called the "impostor syndrome," which leads them to think that they don't belong where they are—that they "snuck in" somehow and aren't nearly as good as everyone else. Law students report this feeling more often than you'd think, and virtually all of the time, they're wrong. They did earn their way into law school, and they are good enough to survive—even thrive—there. If you find yourself thinking that you're the only person who was mistakenly admitted to law school, you might try doing a little reading on that topic, starting here: *http://en.wikipedia.org/wiki/Impostor_syndrome.*[17]

4.2. Your Personal Learning Style

We have one last bit of advice before we get started. What kind of learner are you? Do you retain information better when you draw out charts (visual learner—one of us is heavily into this realm), listen to people talk (aural learner), or work on something hands-on (kinesthetic learner)? Do you need a lot of context before you can start feeling as if you're learning anything at all (contextual learner)?[18] Do you study alone or in a group? If you don't know by now, try a few of the techniques discussed in this book and find out what works best for you. Knowing your learning style can make a difference in how you approach studying in law school. There are all sorts of resources to help you figure out toward which styles you gravitate (*see, e.g., http://www.learning-styles-online.com/overview/*). When you read our chapters on such things as how to study, you'll benefit greatly from knowing what works for you, and then adapting our advice to your own personal style.

5.   One Month Before You Arrive

Do you have your living arrangements set? Do you know all of the ways to get to school (especially if there are traffic challenges where you live)? Do you have a reliable Internet connection? Do you know good places to work out? Eat inexpensively? Decompress (coffee houses, cheap movies, etc.)? Then you're probably all set.

---

[17] Yes, yes, we know. Wikipedia isn't the world's most reliable source (*see, e.g., http://spring.newsvine.com/_news/2006/08/01/307864-stephen-colbert-causes-chaos-on-wikipedia-gets-blocked-from-site*), but sometimes it's useful.

[18] If you're a contextual learner, law school is going to be frustrating for you, because most law school courses have very little context at the beginning. You get a lot of "trees" but no "forest" until almost the end of many courses. Our advice is to find ways to learn context outside of the course materials themselves—hornbooks, commercial outlines, and the like—to give you a bit of comfort as you progress through the course. For information about hornbooks and commercial outlines, see Chapter 5.

6.   A Word About State Bar Admissions Rules

6.1. Generally

We assume that most of you will want to practice law, at least for a while, after you graduate from law school. To practice law in the United States, you'll need to become licensed as an attorney in a particular state. Every state has different rules about applying to sit for the bar examination in that state. Some states are so large and have so many applicants that they require first-year law students to preregister to take the bar exam. (*See http://www.ncbex.org/compre-hensive-guide-to-bar-admissions/*, which lists every state's require-ments.) After you download this guide, pay attention to whether registration as a first-year student is part of a state's requirements.

6.2. Character and Fitness Requirements

Every state's bar association wants to know whether the applicant has demonstrated, through behavior, that he or she can be trusted to take the responsibilities of being a lawyer seriously. Generally speak-ing, you can't sit for a bar examination if you are a convicted felon (at least in most states) or if you've been convicted of a misdemeanor involving moral turpitude (fraud, theft, etc.). But here's some good news: Most bar examiners care more about how someone deals with the "bad marks" on his or her record than on what caused the bad marks in the first place. Even so, all of them will pay very close atten-tion to how an applicant behaved during law school.

Here are some examples of some "stupid law student tricks":[19]

- DWI/DUI convictions during law school.
- Trespassing (e.g., toilet-papering a law professor's house, which is most certainly not an invited act), assault (e.g., during parties, getting into a drunken brawl), and other criminal acts.
- Honor code violations, including plagiarism.

---

[19] À la David Letterman's Stupid Human Tricks. *See http://en.wikipedia.org/wiki/Stupid_Pet_Tricks.*

- Civil disobedience convictions, even though you might feel very good about them.
- Law school applications that don't match the bar applications, especially where convictions are concerned. If your law school application has asked you to list convictions, and you didn't list any, but you listed one on your bar application, the Character and Fitness Committee will be concerned about why your law school application omitted the conviction.[20]

Once you get into law school, a lot of the freedoms that you had before you started disappear. For example, you won't get to use a "reasonable person" standard in comparing your conduct to the behavior of other people.[21] Whether you believe it is fair or not, you are not a "regular person" anymore; you are in law school. You'll have the joy of using a "reasonable law student" standard. Don't make your life worse by engaging in indicia of irresponsibility.

On the other hand, there are times when life will intervene, and you'll have to disclose certain things from your past to the bar examiners. Some states will ask whether you've seen a therapist; others limit their mental health inquiry to whether you have been hospitalized. If you've defaulted on a loan or filed for bankruptcy, the state bars will want to know about that as well. Mental health care, substance abuse problems, and financial difficulties won't prevent you from becoming a lawyer, but you'll need to make sure that you can explain to the state's Character and Fitness Committee[22] how you're handling these problems so that they won't affect your representation of clients.

---

[20] Nancy has seen a flurry of law students rush to the admissions office to amend their applications during law student orientation week, right after the dean mentions this point.

[21] The "reasonable person" standard is the objective standard of behavior against which a particular person's behavior is compared. If a reasonable person would have done—or not done—something, then that particular person should have done, or not done, that same thing.

[22] This committee is charged with determining whether you have the requisite moral character to be licensed as a lawyer. Even if you can pass the bar exam with flying colors, you still have to prove that you're the type of person who can be trusted with client funds, client deadlines, and client confidences.

CHAPTER TWO _____

Orientation: Welcome to Law School

The power of example is very important to people under stress.
—Gen. Sir John Hackett, British Army

1.   Orientation: An Overview

1.1.   Orientation as High School Redux?

Nancy thinks that law school orientation is a lot like the beginning of high school. If you had a great time in high school (as Jeff did), this flashback will be encouraging. If you hated almost all of high school (as Nancy did), this flashback will fill you with dread.

Here's why Nancy thinks that the first year of law school is a lot like high school: You'll have homeroom (your "small section"—a group of fellow law students who will take many of the same courses that you do) and lockers (where you'll keep your heavy law books and study aids); you'll know everyone else's business (especially who's dating whom); and you'll have that same combination of anticipation and fear about your performance.

Jeff doesn't really agree with this "law school is like high school" analogy. Yes, he had a good time in high school. Even so, his first day as an undergraduate in college was nerve-wracking, as were his first few days in law school. As a nontraditional student with more than five years of work experience before both undergraduate school and law school, he didn't really view law school with any real sense of dread. It was more like nervous anticipation about whether he'd be able to keep up with his peers.

Whether you agree with the high-school analogy or not, here's our point: During orientation, and at various points during law school, you'll keep asking yourself if you're cut out for law school. Not to worry. We'll help you survive it.

1.2. A Taxonomy[1] of Law Students

You're likely to see several types of law students in your law school entering class. We're going to classify the most common types for you here, and we'll leave it to you to figure out which type, or combination of types, you are.

The "straight-through" students.   Students who fit into this category didn't take a break between undergraduate or law school, either because they wanted to keep some momentum going or because they didn't have any particular inclination to do anything else in between. Straight-through students are likely to be particularly grade-conscious during the first semester of school because they have always measured their success by their grades. You can generally identify them by the way they introduce themselves to you: "Where did you go to [undergraduate] school? What was your LSAT score?"

Older students.   Older students usually have that slightly befuddled look that underlies a sense of nervous excitement. They are going to law school because they want to be there. They want to become lawyers or to use their legal knowledge in their current jobs. They are, however, a little worried that maybe they've been out of school too long and have forgotten how to study. (That's generally not true, but it's a fairly common concern.) They might be married, have children, be in a relationship, and be working full-time jobs while attending school. They're likely to be wondering how they're going to juggle all of their responsibilities while in school and do them all justice.[2]

---

[1] Taxonomy means classification. If you didn't know what the word meant, we hope that you decided to look it up. The first year of law school involves a lot of looking up unfamiliar words. For example, when Nancy read her first case in Contracts class, the very first word was "Assumpsit." *Hawkins v. McGee,* 146 A. 641 (N.H. 1929). After taking four hours to read four pages, looking up every few words in a law dictionary, Nancy realized that she was in for some hard slogging.

[2] Nancy has a response for this concern when people ask her how she manages to "do it all": "I do it all poorly." That usually shuts them up.

Students who come from a long line of lawyers or who have been paralegals before coming to law school. Typically overconfident, these students are comfortable with legal lingo and will appear to be the most laid–back during orientation. These students might also drop as many "law names" and as much legal jargon as possible in every conversation. Don't be intimidated. These folks might well be just as scared as you are, but will be falling back on having been raised by lawyers to mask the fear.

Students who are the first in their families to go to law school. The opposite of the lineally blessed law students, these students will have to learn the traditions of the law from their experiences in law school. They might come from families who typically become doctors or teachers or from some other background entirely. Their parents might be migrant workers or janitors. Lawyers are nonexistent in these students' family trees.

Second-career students. These students have already had successful careers in other disciplines and are now pursuing law degrees either as a change of pace or as a semiretirement option. Yes, they're usually older than the straight-through students.

"Gunners." You'll be able to recognize gunners by the fact that each of them will have an arm locked in the permanently upright, call-on-me position. Some gunners know what they're talking about; most don't. Only first-year grades will tell the "I know it" from the "I'm faking it" gunners—first-year grades, and the discerning reactions of law professors.

The gunner (an illustration).

Quiet students. The polar opposite end of the student spectrum from the "gunners," quiet students rarely talk in public, either because they are uncomfortable expressing themselves in large groups or because they don't have much that they want to say, preferring to listen to others. Quiet students can do quite well in law school, but they run the risk of not knowing if they're mastering the material before they take their final examinations. Nothing ventured, nothing gained.

Saboteurs.   These students look like human beings, but you can identify them by the way in which they try to undermine the confidence of every one of their fellow students: for example, by misleading their classmates about where to find legal research,[3] by actively participating in gossip, or by preying on their classmates' insecurities. Saboteurs will lie, too: They'll lie about how hard they're working and what grade they got on an assignment or an exam. If you find your confidence drained every time you speak with someone, you're probably interacting with a saboteur.

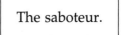

The saboteur.

Braggarts.   Gunners can be completely innocuous, volunteering in class merely to determine if they themselves understand the material. Braggarts, on the other hand, seem to have a malicious streak. They seem compelled to top the stories of their classmates: They need to have worked harder and studied more (while sleeping less) than everyone else in their classes. Pity them. They will be

---

[3] Or, worse yet, by hiding or destroying information that other law students need.

the people who define themselves as attorneys first, humans second. Later on, they'll brag about how many billable hours they've put in, but they won't have any social lives.

Socially awkward students.   These students are just a tad odd. There's nothing really wrong with them. They're nice enough, but they're just not quite "right." Every group has one (or more than one). Try to be nice to these people. Often, they're among the brightest people in the room. Being nice to someone who makes you uncomfortable is good karma.

"Frat boys" and "sorority sisters."   Think Elle Woods in *Legally Blonde*.[4] These students live for the Thursday night "bar reviews" and Friday night pub crawls. There's nothing wrong with relaxing or drinking, but too much of a good thing can lead to disruptions in study schedules, and possibly even substance-abuse-related problems that such students will have to explain to bar examiners later on.

1.3. Orientation Basics

Most orientations give you a pep talk from the dean and the dean of students, a pep talk from the president of the Student Bar Association, a briefing from financial aid, a "demo" class, an introduction to the academic support dean and the career services dean, a meeting with student mentors, and some sort of getting-to-know-your-classmates mixer.

The dean's pep talk.   This portion of orientation usually gives you a feel for the traditions of the school: famous alumni, contributions to society, or educational philosophy. Sometimes the dean will introduce a well-respected alumnus or member of the bar to provide an additional welcome. Listen for any particular themes about the school.

---

[4] MGM (2001).

The pep talk by the dean of students.   This portion of orientation introduces you to the entering statistics of your classmates: where they received their undergraduate degrees, how many of them have advanced degrees, how many of them are from other countries, which ones have unusual hobbies, and so on. The good news is that the dean of students doesn't identify any of these students by name, so you don't have to worry about being "outed" if the dean mentions that someone (you) has a particularly notable hobby. You have two choices during this talk: You can start to feel intimidated by how great everyone else sounds, or you can try to figure out which people you'd like to meet.

The pep talk from the Student Bar Association president.   The SBA president will want you to get involved in law student life: Join some clubs, go to some mixers, volunteer. And you should. But be judicious in choosing what to do. (See Chapter 5.) You can't (and shouldn't) do it all, or you won't have time for your main job, which is surviving and even doing well in law school.

The introduction to the school's honor code.   Some schools have complex honor codes, full of rules and definitions; other schools' codes are akin to the honor code at West Point, which states simply, "A cadet will not lie, cheat, steal, or tolerate those who do."[5] Because lawyers are bound by the ethics rules of the jurisdictions in which they're admitted to practice, law schools want their students to get used to abiding by similar codes. Listen carefully at orientation, as most honor codes require students to report other students' violations, and the failure to report someone else's violation is usually a violation in itself. Determining whether you or a fellow student might have violated the honor code is a painful process, but failing to report a potential violation might actually keep you from sitting for the bar exam after graduation.

The financial aid lecture.   Take this portion of orientation seriously. The debt load for law school graduates can be astronomical, and those six-figure starting salaries are significantly harder to get (and keep) than they once were. The best mantra is still "Live like a

---

[5] *http://www.usma.edu/Committees/Honor/Info/main.htm.*

The getting-to-know-your-classmates mixer (and the first few weeks of getting to know them in class).   Contrary to his extroverted and enthusiastic wife, Jeff is a poster child for the introvert law student. If you are like him, meeting your classmates can be far more of an ordeal than a pleasure. Let's be honest: When you walk into a room with more than 100 brand new law students (most of whom are at least as smart as you are), you'll see lots of very nervous, big-ego, Type A personalities milling about and trying to stand out in the crowd. That environment is not conducive to making friends easily. Even so, Jeff managed to make many acquaintances and a few good friends within his class, some of whom he still keeps in touch with more than 20 years later.

For Jeff, it was easier to hang back a bit in class, answering questions when asked and making sure that when he volunteered something in class, his comments had a purpose. (Plenty of your classmates will be happy to fill the room with their voices. You know the type. They were in your undergraduate classes, too, but there were fewer of them there.) Mark our words: Just because they're talking doesn't mean they know what they're talking about. After about ten days or two weeks, Jeff had spotted a few folks with similar backgrounds to his (former military or law enforcement), and he felt comfortable going for coffee and meals with them. His comfortable crowd included some bright people with whom he wanted to try to work (meaning "study"). They seemed to have a better grasp on some things that he was not getting as quickly as he wanted.

You might find, as we did, that the people you meet during orientation become the people with whom you have lunch on your first day, and the second day, and the day after that. That group of people might in turn morph into your study group. More important, that group might morph into your best friends in law school.

Upperclass law students (students who have finished their first year of law school).   We'll offer a few words about upperclass students here. Our experiences with upperclass students were almost uniformly positive. Jeff was a member of the student government as a first-year student, a member of his school's competitive moot court advocacy team as a second-year student, and the Executive Editor of the Law Review as a third-year student. In every one of those capacities, he had the opportunity to interact with upperclass students at school, and he believes that the interaction worked to his benefit, as they steered him in the right direction at almost every branch in the road. (If you don't have to reinvent the wheel, why should you?)

Mind you, not all the information that upperclass students give you will work for you. Listen to everyone's advice, and then carefully decide which advice to take and which advice to ignore. Just because someone is an upperclass student does not mean that he or she knows anything.

One more thought along these lines: You are not going to like all of your classmates or the upperclass students that you meet. (Nor they, you.) Not to worry. As with your undergraduate institution, you are generally not going to be required to have frequent and continuous contact with everyone in your class. But do yourself a favor and try not to alienate too many folks too early. There's always time to tick someone off later. One of Nancy's favorite sayings is attributed to Oscar Wilde: "A gentleman is one who never hurts anyone's feelings unintentionally." And the law school community, like the legal community, is smaller than you'd guess.

1.4. Do You Need Any Disability Accommodations?

If you have needed disability accommodations in the past, you should seek out the dean of students now—during orientation—and start the process for getting accommodations before classes start in earnest. The school might want you to be tested by one of the doctors that it uses, so the process could take time. Forewarned is forearmed.

2.   A Few Introductory Words About Stress and Law School

2.1. Surviving the Stress

Law school can be a *very* stressful[8] experience. In the context of our discussion here, stress is a negative and should be reduced or

---

[8] Stress is both a good and a bad thing. The right amount of stress can make you alert and ready for battle. Too much stress, though, is bad. It leads to poor

eliminated if possible. Performing well in school requires several skill sets, not the least of which is the ability to overcome or control the stressful law school environment.

2.1.1.   Where does the stress come from?

Stress in law school is, at least from our perspective, both self-created and externally generated. The self-created stress arises from not only the desire to do your best in each class, but also the quest to do well as compared with your peers. In part, the stress comes from approaching a new discipline (law) while learning a new way of thinking (legal reasoning). If you're used to the step-by-step method of legal reasoning, then you won't feel particularly stressed, but if you're like we were, learning "the law" while learning how to "think like lawyers" is stress *squared*.

Doing well in school can have significant financial and status implications for a law student. Some firms will only interview the top X percent of a class; top graduates have opportunities and options open to them that people lower in the class won't have for several years after graduation, if ever. Consequently, doing well in school *is* important to your future.[9]

The external stressors of law school are also lurking around virtually every corner. They come from, in no particular order, interpersonal and relationship (friends and family) issues,[10] family pressure to do well, the obvious financial rewards of landing a good job, the status of making law review, the potential job opportunities from doing well in school—for example, a clerkship with a

---

decision making and has adverse consequences over the long run. For purposes of this book, when we discuss stress and stressors, we are talking about the destructive form of stress that leads to difficulty in making decisions, angry outbursts, forgetfulness, low energy levels, constant worrying, propensity for stupid mistakes, trouble getting along with others, withdrawing from others, hiding from responsibilities, and carelessness. *See, e.g.,* FM 21-76, Army Survival Manual, Section 2-3 at 6 (2002), available at *http://www.equipped.com/fm21-76.htm.*

[9] Nonetheless, even if you don't have top grades, what really counts is whether you're learning the material and learning how to analyze issues. In the long run, grades are supposed to *reflect* knowledge, not be a substitute for it.

[10] Two of Jeff's law school classmates divorced shortly after graduating from school; numerous boyfriends and girlfriends were lost (and replacements sometimes found) during school.

federal judge—and the potential hostile reactions of classmates who might not understand why you're taking school so seriously.[11]

People don't get admitted into law school unless they performed well—in some cases spectacularly well—while at their undergraduate institution. Literally speaking, law school students represent some of the very best students from their individual undergraduate institutions. We raise this issue not to make law school look more daunting than it is, but to emphasize that the student talent pool in law school is considerably deeper than that found in most undergraduate schools. Moreover, law students tend to be a competitive bunch (much like athletes). To us, competition is neither good nor bad—it just *is*. But your tendency to be competitive will ramp up the stress level for you, especially if you want to be at the top of your class.[12]

2.1.2.   What should you do about the stress?

There are many ways to mitigate the stressors found in law school. Many use the plentiful social opportunities in school as a mechanism to blow off steam and maintain a balanced life. If you socialize only in moderation, you'll probably be in good shape.

---

[11] Several of Jeff's classmates gave him grief and accused him of taking life much too seriously during his first year in law school. They simply didn't understand what he'd already figured out: What you do in life and law school matters. He took school seriously, because he knew that his performance in school was going to affect his life after he got his law degree. Eventually the remainder of his class figured it out, too. During the early part of his third year, he already had a clerkship offer in hand from one of the justices of the Ohio Supreme Court, and one of those same guys came over to him and apologized for what he had said roughly 16 months earlier; he now understood. He had socialized a bit too much and his grades and class rank had suffered because of it. He had no job, no real job prospects, and was looking his student loans square in the face with no way to pay them back. The lesson? What you do in school matters, so understand it and plan for it. It's a marathon, not a sprint.

[12] Nancy, who always loved being at the top of her class as an undergraduate, spent the first few weeks of law school reassuring herself that it was perfectly okay *not* to be at the top of her class in law school after getting to know some people who were considerably smarter than she was. She figured that there were always going to be people who were taller than she was, too, and that if she wasn't going to get bent out of shape about being shorter than some (okay, most) people, she couldn't very well be upset because she was not as smart as some people, either.

Some folks use their family, friends, or study groups as a mechanism to vent their feelings and reduce the stress. (Just make sure that your venting isn't one-sided; your friends and family also have their own stress and will need you to listen to them sometimes.) Both of us used working out as our primary means of reducing stress. During school, Jeff continued to strength–train and play racquetball, tennis, and golf, simply expanding his pool of participants to include his new classmates. Nancy became a power-lifter, working out after her most stressful class each day.

We recommend a combination of all of the above. An active social life in school is necessary for finding friends and learning about your classmates, many of whom will be colleagues after law school. A healthy social life also provides you with opportunities to meet potential study group members. The key is moderation in all of the things that you do outside of school.

For both of us, law school was *not* an all-encompassing quest to be first in our class. (By definition, being first in your class is a function of how well you do *and* how well your classmates do, so part of the quest is automatically out of your control.) We were nervous and wanted to do the best that we could in school. If doing our best happened to place us high in our class, fine; if not, then, well, so be it.

2.1.3. Keep a lifeline to the outside world

Whatever you do, you need to have contact with people outside of the law school. (We call these people "normal people.") Do *not* completely abandon your friends from your life before law school.

Granted, you'll likely be living in a new city, and you might know virtually no one outside of school. You'll be making new friends inside the school; after all, you spend nearly all your time with these folks. But you need to do your best not to get isolated from the real world. Law school will give you tunnel vision and a skewed view of the world. The real world will keep you honest and give you appropriate feedback about your perspective. Jeff was fortunate enough to go to school in a place where he still had non-law-school friends. His friends kept him balanced and confronted him with a hefty dose of reality when he needed it. It is not easy to balance your law school life with your "real" life, but you'll be considerably better off if you can do it.

3.   Your Checklist for Law School

3.1. Books That You Should Have

- A law dictionary.
- Your textbooks.
- Books that will help you survive law school. Obviously, we think that ours will help, and we like some others as well. These include Ann L. Iijima, *The Law Student's Pocket Mentor: From Surviving to Thriving* (2007) and Kimm Alayne Walton, Lazar Emanuel, & Eric S. Lambert, *Strategies & Tactics for the First Year Law Student* (2004). Wait to get any study aids until you've been in school a little while, so that you can figure out which study aids, if any, will work for you.

3.2. Other Things to Have

- *A laptop.* You might not be allowed to take your laptop into class—some professors prohibit their use in class, and others don't care—but laptops are useful for outlining, doing legal research outside the law library, and other nice things like maintaining e-mail contact with the outside world.
- *Your first-day class assignments.* Unless you want to channel Elle Woods again, find out where your first-day assignments are posted ahead of time and read them. Yes, Elle eventually graduated with honors. But *her* Harvard was a mythical place with a class size of 50. Don't be fooled.
- *Books to inspire you.* Sometimes, you'll need to read (or just hold) a book about why lawyers are important. Here are some of our favorites:
  - Anthony Lewis, *Gideon's Trumpet* (1989).
  - Jonathan Harr, *A Civil Action* (1996).
  - Richard Kluger, *Simple Justice: The History of Brown v. Board of Education and Black America's Struggle for Equality* (2004).
  - Harper Lee, *To Kill a Mockingbird* (1982 ed.).
  - John Grisham, *The Innocent Man* (2007).
- *A sense of humor.* Trust us, you'll need one.

4.   Be Careful How Much You Borrow

When Nancy served on the American Bar Association's Commission on Loan Repayment and Forgiveness, she was horrified to learn that the average debt load for law students, back in 2003, was more than $80,000—just for law school debt. That figure has increased in the years since the Commission issued its report. (You can find the report at *www.abanet.org/legalservices/sclaid/lrap/downloads/lrapfinalreport.pdf.*) If you have significant undergraduate debt as well, that debt, plus your law school debt, will start to come due six months after you graduate from law school. More important, that debt is nondischargeable in bankruptcy, except in truly unusual situations. In other words, once you owe educational debt, you owe it until you pay it back.

Many law students assume that they'll be able to pay off their debt easily by getting one of those six-figure jobs that they've read about. Not everyone gets one of those six-figure jobs, though, and even those who do still have to deal with taxes, rent, dry cleaning those nifty suits they have to wear to work, getting those fancy shirts pressed, eating take-out food because they never get home from work in time to buy food or cook, and paying other people to walk their dogs for them. You get our point. Life for people earning six-figure salaries is no bed of roses, and even if they love their jobs, there's no guarantee that they won't get laid off.

The remaining recent law graduates who are making nice, but not exorbitant, livings, might really have to struggle to pay rent (or a mortgage) and their monthly loans. Our point is that you should keep your borrowing to a minimum so that you don't have to scramble to make ends meet after you graduate.

5.   What if You Want to Do Public Interest Work After You Graduate?

Our first piece of advice is that you find a law school that gives you a free ride in exchange for the promise to do public interest work after graduation (scholarships, grants, etc.). If you can't get a free ride, then choose a good school with as low a tuition bill as humanly possible, or one with a very good LRAP. The ABA has gathered information about LRAPs at *http://www.abanet.org/ legalservices/sclaid/lrap/home.html*. As we mentioned earlier, you can find information about the Federal LRAP program at *http:// www.abanet.org/legalservices/sclaid/lrap/federallrap.html*. Some states have enacted LRAP statutes as well, and one of the best Web sites to help you do some research is at *http://www.equaljusticeworks.org/ resources/student-debt-relief/*. Public interest work can be among the most rewarding work that you can do as a lawyer, but the way to enjoy it is to be able to survive on the salary that you're likely to earn.

CHAPTER THREE

Some Universal Truths

If there is not the war, you don't get the great general; if there is not a great occasion, you don't get a great statesman; if Lincoln had lived in a time of peace, no one would have known his name.

—President Theodore Roosevelt

There are certain issues that will remain constant throughout law school. These include collegiality and its close cousin, etiquette; handling stereotyping in law school; the care and feeding of romantic relationships; career-limiting moves associated with social networking and the Internet; and favorite law professor "games." We'll cover each of these topics and then close the chapter with some answers to frequently asked questions.

1.   Collegiality and Etiquette

Your professional reputation as a lawyer starts at law school orientation, not at graduation. Law school deans used to tell students at orientation to "look to your left, look to your right—two of the three of you will be gone before the year is out." Back in the days when law schools tended to have open admissions and then flunk out a significant portion of their first-year students, that advice might have been true. Now, however, if you look to your left and right, you should visualize future colleagues. These are the people who will be working with you or referring clients to you. (They might also become your future clients[1] or might be in a position to assist you with future employment opportunities.)

We shouldn't need to say it, but we will: Be a jerk now, and your classmates will remember it long after you've all graduated. Be nice to your classmates—and civil to the annoying ones—and you've preserved your options. You're well on your way to

---

[1] And one of them might even become your "significant other."

building a good reputation. Besides, karma is a bad thing to waste and virtually impossible to re-create.

Mind you, don't be civil only to your classmates. You should be nice (or at least civil) to everyone in the law school (and university) community, from the support staff to the president of the university. You're about to enter the world of the professional, and professionals are privileged people. Privileged people need to behave properly, and that means behaving in a way that would make your parents proud.

1.1. Help Each Other Out

Share outlines. Help each other understand parts of a course that might be difficult.[2] Listen when someone's struggling. Your school might curve grades, but when you're in the final, you're really only competing against yourself. In many ways, law school is like golf. The best people are those who don't cheat, who behave responsibly and politely, and who don't engage in temper tantrums. Many years after law school, people will reach out to their classmates who were the nice ones during law school. They'll leave the rats out in the cold.

One of the most rewarding things about being associated with law schools is watching how willing most law students are to help each other. We've seen friends of new parents take turns watching babies while the parents attend class. We've watched law students with classmates deployed in the military assemble care packages. We've even watched classmates talk each other out of quitting (and offer to help each other catch up). As we've said before, karma is an amazing thing. Reach out, and you really will be rewarded for it—even if it's just by feeling better about yourself and about the world in which you live.

1.2. Don't Be an Insufferable Braggart

One of Nancy's favorite memories from law school is studying for first-semester exams in the law school dorm with her friends.

---

[2] Explaining something to a classmate is one of the best ways to learn it yourself.

Someone else wandered in and said, "Ask me anything!" The reply from her group: "Sure. Would you leave?" Jeff concurs: Bragging about how prepared you are for a test is annoying to nearly everyone. When grades come out, the truth is obvious, and lots of braggarts slink off into the corner. This same rule applies to your outside friends (those people who aren't lawyers and aren't in law school). They already know that you're in law school. Don't remind them constantly of that fact, of how hard law school is, or of how wonderful you are because you're in law school. If you do, our only good news is that you won't have to worry about having non-law-school friends for very long.

1.3. Have Mercy on the Awkward, the Stressed, the Cranky, and the Shy

Everyone at your law school deserves to be there, but some people are more comfortable being there than are others. There will be days when you'll feel out of place yourself, so try to remember that others can have bad days, too.

2. Stereotypes (Either on the "Giving" or "Receiving" End)

Malcolm Gladwell's book *Blink*[3] discusses how quickly people make judgments about other people and situations. That ability to make snap judgments is hard-wired into human nature, and it's a way of helping us decide whether to fight or run away when we're on unfamiliar turf. We all make snap judgments all the time.

Your classmates (and, yes, your professors) will make snap judgments, too. Maybe someone will look like a surfer dude, or a frat boy, or a bookworm. If you're the person being judged, it might take a while for others' reactions to you to change. (If you're the one doing the judging, be aware that you might be wrong.)

For example, Jeff looks fierce, with his short, militaristic haircut and his perfect posture. He also appears standoffish at first, but that's not because he's stuck up. It's actually because he's rather

---

[3] Malcolm Gladwell, *Blink: The Power of Thinking Without Thinking* (2005).

shy.[4] People frequently make assumptions about him, but those assumptions are often wrong.

There's another type of assumption that can hurt some law students. It's a syndrome called stereotype threat.[5] In a situation in which there are not very many of a group of people—such as women or people of color or older people—members of that group might feel as if they aren't just performing for themselves, but that they're representing their entire group. That adds an extra burden to their educational experience, especially when the members of the group are told that they're not expected to perform as well as their majority peers.

If you find yourself on the receiving end of a message that says that "your kind" is not supposed to do well in school, we have this advice:

- As tempting as it will be to punch the person delivering the message, don't. You'd have to explain yourself to the members of the Character and Fitness Committee of whatever bar you plan to take (not to mention explaining yourself to local law enforcement).

- Remember that you have as much right to be in law school as everyone else who was admitted to your entering class.

- Don't try to "represent" your entire group. (First off, you're not the member of just one group. You're a member of several groups. For example, Nancy is a short, female, Jewish, ballroom-dancing law professor who writes in three distinct areas of the law. Try to pin *her* down to just one group!)

- Focus on you, and what you're learning in law school. The best response to being "dissed" is to succeed.

---

[4] You'd be surprised at how many litigators are shy outside of their work personas.

[5] *See, e.g., http://reducingstereotypethreat.org/; see also* Adam D. Galinsky, Leigh Thompson, & Laura Kray, *Taking Stereotypes out of Stereotype Threat: The Effect of Role-Based Expectations,* available at *http://ssrn.com/abstract=399620.*

3.   The Care and Feeding of Romantic Relationships

If you've come into law school with an active romance, and if your romance is healthy, then you'll want to make the effort to nurture and protect it. Take some time away from your studies and spend that time with your partner. Talk about things other than law school. Ask about your partner's day. Try to listen.

If you've come into law school with a dysfunctional relationship, end it. End it *now*. You'll have enough stress in your life during law school without also having to deal with late-night dramas, nasty screaming matches, passive-aggressive warfare, and low self-esteem.

If you're starting a romance during law school, just realize that everyone's going to know about it. There are no secrets in law school, just as there weren't any in high school. If the relationship makes it all the way to graduation, great; if it doesn't, everyone at school will know, probably within seconds of the breakup. Nothing's more efficient than the law school gossip network.

4.   Career-Limiting Moves That Come With Social Networking and the Internet

We'll talk about this issue more when we talk about your resume in connection with getting a summer job, but for now, we want to make it clear: The Internet is *forever*. Every picture of you drinking at a party, every nasty nonanonymous post that you've put on someone's Facebook page, every dumb thing that has been captured in cyberspace is there for all time. Employers can find all of those dumb things. So can bar examiners. So can admissions committees. Be careful now about what's out there.

Don't believe us? Why don't you Google the story of a young Boston lawyer who accepted a job, then broke her promise to the law firm. The law firm was understandably miffed, having already prepared for her start date. The young lawyer claimed, in essence, that an oral employment contract was worth the paper on which it was printed.[6] The law firm chastised her for her "immatur[e] and

---

[6] Irony intended. And why wasn't she paying attention in her Contracts class?

quite unprofessional" behavior, to which she replied, in an e-mail that became viral on the Internet:

> ————Original Message————
> From: Dianna Abdala
> To: William A. Korman
> Sent: Monday, February 06, 2006 4:28 PM
> Subject: Re: Thank you
> bla bla bla[7]

Every time Ms. Abdala gets Googled, she'll have to explain this story to future employers.[8] You don't want to have to endure this type of permanent history.[9]

5.   Nancy's Favorite Story About Miscommunication in E-Mails

Although you know what tone of voice you're using when you write an e-mail, the reader can't hear your tone of voice when receiving that e-mail. English is a funny language, and sometimes the most well-meaning of e-mails can cause unfortunate misunderstandings.

What happens, for example, when you send an e-mail, the recipient never gets it, and she asks you to send it again? Well, you'd send the e-mail again, right? And you'd want to let the recipient know that you sent it. So in your warm, fuzzy mind,

---

[7] *http://abcnews.go.com/Nightline/story?id=1635684.*

[8] And, for that matter, to future dates.

[9] When we were children, we were often warned by school authority figures that anything bad that we'd done would go "on our permanent record." We never believed that there was such a thing as a "permanent record." We were correct then, because the Internet hadn't yet been invented. But now the Internet *is* that "permanent record."

Don't believe us about permanence? Nancy's dad was surfing the Internet one day in 2009 and turned up a letter that he'd written to *Time Magazine* back in 1960 when he was a graduate student. That's *1960*, long before computers were in homes, and long before letters to the editor were inputted into computers for later use. So even the things that you did before you were aware that they *could* be on your permanent record are, in fact, on that record.

you're saying that you've sent the e-mail again. But you're typing something that will send a very different message: "I resent the e-mail."

You meant that you re-sent it. But that's not what the e-mail looks like, is it? Lesson: If you find yourself getting angry about an e-mail, ask yourself if the sender is actually trying to make you angry, or whether it's possible that the e-mail might be miscommunicating what the sender intended to say.

One more bit of advice about e-mails: When you're angry, your fingers will start itching to press "send" on an e-mail nastygram. If you want to avoid that awful feeling of regret at an intemperate e-mail, just leave the "To" field blank. Write the darn e-mail to get your anger out of your system.[10] Save it in drafts. As long as the "To" field is blank, you can't send off your missive of invective to anyone, and you'll have an opportunity to ask yourself if you really, really want to send it.

6.   Favorite Law Professor "Games"

You're likely to experience several of these games during law school, and you might experience feelings of abject stupidity while "playing." Don't. Contrary to popular belief, most professors really aren't trying to make you feel dumb.

- "Hide the ball." When a law student comes up with the perfect answer too early in Socratic questioning, the law professor rejects the correct answer as incorrect, only to accept the exact same answer twenty minutes later.

- "Guess what I'm thinking." The professor asks a question that she thinks will trigger only one answer, but students keep giving her several acceptable answers that she must reject until she gets the only one that she wants.

- "Target of inquiry." Student asks a simple question, and the professor then uses that student's inquiry to launch a full

---

[10] Nancy always starts off the body of her angry draft e-mails with "Dear Mush-for-Brains." That salutation soothes her enormously.

Socratic inquiry on some other topic—but to that same student.

- "Maintaining the Official Law Professor's License." Student asks a question. Instead of answering, the professor responds with, "Well, Mr./Ms. X, what do *you* think the answer is?"[11]

7.   FAQs

7.1.   Does It Matter Where I Sit in Class?

Assuming that your professors don't assign you to a seat, then where you sit really doesn't matter. What matters is that you need to be able to see and hear each of your professors and your classmates. Be aware, however, that the professors can see you talking to your classmates, passing notes (if laptops are prohibited), IMing each other (if laptops are allowed), laughing, and reading the newspaper or magazines. It only hurts some professors' feelings, but it irritates virtually all of them.[12] In one of Jeff's classes, the professor had a habit of calling on the students who didn't seem to be paying attention (reading the newspapers or talking to classmates became a question "magnet").[13]

Sometimes, you'll notice that professors have "front-row blindness" or "left-" or "right-side" blindness, where they tend not to call on students who are sitting in those areas. If you are sitting in one of those areas and you want to ask a question, you might have to try a little harder to get the professor to notice you.

---

[11] Nancy is convinced that she will lose her license to be a law professor if she doesn't ask at least one student per course per semester this question.

[12] Now, aren't you glad that grades are usually anonymous?

[13] Nancy had an annoying habit of her own in law school: When she got bored, she simply left the classroom. She admits now how rude this behavior was, but she thinks it was better than distracting her classmates by chatting with them or rattling the newspaper. She also thinks that she became a law professor in part to repent for her rude law student behavior, à la Hayley Mills in *The Trouble With Angels* (Columbia Pictures 1966).

7.2. If I Really, Really Have to Go to the Bathroom During Class, Is It Okay if I Get Up and Leave?

Try not to put yourself in that position frequently, but if you have to go, go. Law professors aren't the bathroom police. But leaving class to, for example, take a smoking break, answer a cell phone call, stretch your legs, and so on is only going to make your professor think that you're either a slacker or that you don't think that his or her class is very important. Will such behavior hurt your grade? Not necessarily, unless classroom participation is a significant percentage of your grade. But don't count on getting any glowing recommendations from that professor.

If you have a medical condition that requires you to leave the classroom frequently, let your professors know about that condition before class, and try to sit near an exit so that you don't disturb your classmates too much.

7.3. If My Readings for Class Have Footnotes, Do I Need to Read the Footnotes, Too?

Yes.[14]

7.4. Do I Need to Look Up All of the Cases, Statutes, and Other Material Mentioned in Those Footnotes and Read Those as Well?

No.

7.5. What Harm Is There in Surfing the Web in Class or IMing My Friends if I'm Bored?

No matter how good you are at multitasking, you're not learning very much if you're surfing the Web, checking e-mail, or IMing

---

[14] Some footnotes are very important. *See United States v. Carolene Products Co.*, 304 U.S. 144, 152 n.4 (1938) (trust us, you'll get to that footnote in Constitutional Law). Other footnotes are useful or just plain fun (*see generally* many of ours).

your friends. And you're probably distracting those around you. We both believe that you might as well just skip class entirely if you're going to spend your time in class pretending that you're paying attention. At least then, you wouldn't have to worry about being called on while you're playing on your computer.[15] And for goodness' sake, have the common decency not to look at tasteless or pornographic sites while you're in class. The old saying "Better to keep your mouth shut and be thought a fool than to open it and remove all doubt" could well be updated to say, "Better to keep your laptop shut and be thought a jerk than to leave it open and remove all doubt."

7.6. If I Hate My Law School, Can I Transfer After My First Year?

Probably not. If your target law school (the one to which you want to transfer) needs to fill some additional seats in its upper-level classes, it might consider a few transfer students, but it will only consider those at the very top of their first-year class at their "home" school. So don't matriculate at a school expecting to transfer to another school in your second year.

There could be several drawbacks to transferring to another school. Your target school will probably not accept your first-year GPA from the school that you're planning to leave, so you'll lose any advantage that you had from a high GPA. Instead, your grades might transfer just as "pass" grades, which means that you might find it more difficult to participate in second-year activities, such as law review or moot court teams, if the selection process for those activities requires a certain first-year GPA or class rank. You could lose any scholarships that you had during your first year, because most scholarships aren't transferable from school to school. And, not surprisingly, you'll have to find a new set of friends at your new school.

On the other hand, if you do decide to transfer—and you're accepted at your target school—take advantage of all of the

---

[15] One of Nancy's favorite games to play in class is "walk up to someone who's IMing to see how long it takes to notice that she's *right there*." See the earlier section on "Favorite Law Professor Games."

opportunities that your new school has to offer. If that school is better regarded than your "home" school, then you will likely have more opportunities for interviewing, and more doors might open for you in other ways as well. Investigate joining the school's law review and its moot court team—and agitate to get transfer students the ability to join those teams, if necessary;[16] get to know the career services office; and plan to apply for judicial clerkships in your last year of law school. After all, you've demonstrated your ability in your first year of law school. Why lose momentum after you transfer?

7.7.   What if I Want to Live Somewhere After Graduation Other Than Where My Law School Is Located?

If you're a student at a "national" law school, you'll have many options; if you go to a well-regarded regional school, you should be fine as well, but you'll have to do more legwork to get leads on jobs in your desired geographic area. You might consider becoming a "transient" student during your third year. (No, that doesn't mean that you become homeless. A transient student visits at another law school but gets her degree from her "home" law school.) The advantage of being a transient student at a school in your desired region is that you can use that school's career services contacts for finding a job.

---

[16] Agitate nicely, though. Don't be a jerk about the issue. Good lawyers can be insistent without being annoying.

CHAPTER FOUR

The First Two Weeks

The battlefield is a scene of constant chaos. The winner will be the one who controls that chaos, both his own and the enemy's.

—**Napoleon Bonaparte**

1.   Managing the Workload

Jeff is the first to admit that he worked harder and studied more in law school than he ever did as an undergraduate student.[1] Not only was the material sometimes more difficult for him to absorb, but the mandatory readings were easily two or three times longer than he had seen before, as in hundreds of pages of material for each class. Even so, he managed to maintain a regular physical training regimen and an only somewhat limited social life.

Both of us believe that, as with training for any kind of sport, you need to manage your class schedule and studying workload to allow yourself adequate time for rest and recovery, as well as having a semblance of a life. We had the opportunity to watch many of our classmates panic during the middle of a semester, burn the candle at both ends for long periods, and literally study themselves into exhaustion. Our motto is "Work early and avoid the rush at the end."[2]

Twenty-hour to twenty-four-hour days are fine once in a while, but they can't comprise the foundational basis of your studying regimen. Your body and mind simply can't tolerate such stress over time. Under such a schedule, body and mind will break down and fail you at the most inopportune time possible (during exams).

---

[1] For Nancy, it was the other way around. She studied all the time as an undergraduate, and although she worked hard in law school, she thought that her undergraduate workload was more difficult.

[2] This is the corollary to the sarcastic phrase that Jeff and his friends used in law school to explain the constant state of panic that seemed to envelop several of their classmates: "Panic early and avoid the rush during finals."

Eventually, you will acclimate to the increased workload and become more efficient in preparing for class. Additionally, you'll figure out how much time you'll actually *need* to prepare adequately for class. Everyone is different; the level of class preparation that worked for each of us might well not work for you. Significantly, your preparation levels will likely vary from class to class. Some topics are going to prove easier for you than others.

Although we didn't know each other in law school, we have since discovered that we were both "code geeks." We loved every code course that we took (e.g., Contracts, the Uniform Commercial Code, Secured Transactions, Evidence, etc.). Those were the classes for which preparation time was a breeze. Conversely, classes like Constitutional Law, Real Property, and Administrative Law took more effort and preparation and study time for each of us. One of our best friends was a Property whiz. Go figure.

A word of caution: There is a clear difference between doing what's *necessary* to be prepared and doing what's *possible* (i.e., extra) to do. Knowing the difference between the two is essentially what separates first-semester, first-year law students (who seem to want to read every case mentioned in every footnote) and upperclass students. The other main difference between first-year and upperclass law students is class preparation efficiency, and the use and reliance on third-party topic-matter materials (also known as study guides).

Jeff was much more rigidly organized than Nancy was in terms of scheduling. As you'll see a bit later in this chapter and in Appendix A, he used a written calendar to help plan his month, week, and daily school-related activities.[3] The calendar showed all of the classes as

---

[3] If you're an über-planner, you might consider a semester-long calendar as well. Such a calendar will remind you when assignments are due.

well as additional information. The daily calendar showed each class on that day, the period that he planned to use to prepare for that class, the period that he would use to write his outline for that class (we'll talk about outlining in Chapter 5), and the period that he'd use to study the outlines that he had prepared. Eventually, he needed a less formal calendar, but he is a chart guy, so writing it down was what he did to stay organized. (Anyone who knows Nancy knows that she relies on the organizational skills of others to keep her on track.) You might not need such a formalized process as a written calendar, but having one freed Jeff from the panic that he was going to forget to do something. The calendar let him glance to see if he was staying current with everything that needed to be done.

1.1. "Do I Need to Know This?" Why Law School Is Not Like Your Undergraduate Education

Want to give a law professor an honest-to-goodness nervous tic? All you have to do is raise your hand in class and ask the question that didn't seem to bother your lecturers in undergraduate classes (although it probably did bother the professors there, too): "Do I need to know this?"

Of course you need to know what the professor is teaching you. Law school is a professional school. You're learning how to be a lawyer, and every course that you take—*every* course, especially your research and writing courses—adds to the panoply of skills that you'll need to be a competent lawyer. Would you want a doctor or an engineer to ask her professors if she needs to know what they're teaching *her*?

Because everything in the upper level of law school builds on the first-year courses, you really need to make sure that you understand what you're being taught. If you're not following most of the class discussion, drop by your professor's office during office hours or make an appointment for a longer visit. Don't wait until the end of the semester, under the assumption that everything will fall into place. And don't waste time hoping for a miracle. Law school might not be rocket science,[4] but it does take some hard work.

---

[4] We have a friend, Randy Morgan, who *is* a rocket scientist (currently working in Mission Control for the International Space Station), so we check with

1.2. A Word About Reading Cases

Many of your first-year courses will involve a significant amount of common-law (case law) instruction.[5] Learning what the law is from reading a lot of cases is like looking for numbers in those color-blindness tests that have all of those dots in them,[6] or those darn Magic Eye 3D images.[7] Some people are better at weeding out the unnecessary parts of the case than others are, and reading cases is a skill that gets better with practice.

The point of learning law through cases is to see how a court applies a rule of law (or applies an exception to the rule) to a particular set of facts. No rule is 100 percent easy to apply, because there are always holes in drafting a rule. Take, for example, the speed limit on an urban street. If the speed limit on the street is 35 miles per hour, that's the "rule." But what if the weather's really awful? Then 35 miles per hour would be unreasonably fast, and an exception to the rule ("Drive 35 unless the weather makes driving 35 unreasonable") would kick in. On the other hand, what if you'd sliced your hand open while making a sandwich and needed to get to an emergency room in a hurry? Then keeping to a 35-mile-per-hour speed limit would be potentially detrimental to your health, and another exception to the speed limit would be "except in an emergency." So if you were a judge, faced with determining whether someone should be convicted of violating the speed limit, you'd have the rule (35 MPH) and two very different exceptions to the rule to apply. Moreover, you wouldn't know all of the facts—just the ones that the lawyers on either side of the case chose to present to you. Therefore, your opinion would be based on your application of the rule to the particular facts that you (or the jury) found, based on the evidence presented in that particular case.

Now you can see why the same rule of law might produce different results in different cases. The facts might be different, or the lawyers might simply have argued them differently (or

---

him from time to time to determine what is, and isn't, rocket science. Law school isn't. We've checked with Randy.

[5] Unless you're in law school in Louisiana, which is a civil law (statutory) state.

[6] See http://www.toledo-bend.com/colorblind/Ishihara.asp.

[7] See http://www.magiceye.com/3dfun/stwkdisp.shtml.

argued for different rules to apply). Deducing what a legal rule should be, based on reading the cases in your textbook, is a tricky proposition. That's why we're code geeks. Statutes, to us, are easier to understand.

1.3. Reading Statutes

Even code geeks have problems reading statutes. Generally speaking, statutes are horribly written. They thrive on passive voice, seem to love double negatives, and seem intent on hiding their true meaning from the average human being. It's embarrassing (at least to us) to realize that most statutes are crafted by lawyers. We sometimes think lawyers who draft statutes poorly do it on purpose to make regular folks think that they need a lawyer to understand the law. But that's only in our more cynical moments.

There are, however, some fairly simple rules that will help you glean the wheat from the chaff of a statute. Some states, like Texas, make life considerably easier by statutorily imposing rules to be used in interpreting the statutory provisions. (Yes, you read that right: There are statutes that tell you how to read statutes.) Other states use the case law to impose the virtually identical rules that Texas imposes by statute.[8] The following are the rules that Jeff used (and continues to use to this day) for interpreting statutory provisions:

- If a term has a specific definition (e.g., a statutory definition or industry standard), use that definition when applying the term.
- If a term is not otherwise defined, give it its ordinary meaning.
- Do not read statutory provisions in isolation; they must be read in conjunction with other provisions in such a way that all of the provisions, when read together, make logical sense.

---

[8] *See* V.T.C.A., Government Code §311.001 et seq. (Acts 1985, 69th Leg., ch. 479, §1, eff. Sept. 1, 1985) (Texas Code Construction Act).

- Don't engage in semantic gymnastics[9] to glean the meaning of a statutory provision (you shouldn't contort the statutory language to obtain the meaning; lawyers sometimes try to contort case law or statutory language to obtain a specifically sought-after result).
- If statutory language is clear and unambiguous, don't use interpretation rules to interpret the language of the provision—just apply the clear and unambiguous language.
- When you're not sure how various provisions work together, make a flowchart. (If you've never seen a flowchart, take a look at the one we've done in Chapter 5, Section 5.2.2.)
- If earlier versions of a specific statute are available and you're permitted to use them to interpret the statute (typically, case law will tell you whether you can use earlier versions for interpretive purposes), then use those earlier versions to figure out what the legislature meant when it amended the statute (that's the statute's evolutionary legislative history).

---

[9] Think we made up the phrase "semantic gymnastics"? Au contraire!

At first blush, appellant's argument concerning the requirement of consecutive notice has merit. However, appellant's emphasis on the meaning of the word "consecutive" merely demonstrates an exercise in semantic gymnastics. The statute requires published notice once a week for three consecutive weeks before the sale. There is no requirement that these three notices be published immediately before the sale date. The notices themselves must be consecutive to one another. Appellant's inclusion of the actual sale date as a factor of this consecutive series is neither statutorily required nor equitably necessary.

Transamerica Financial Services v. Fitzgerald, 1982 WL 5839, *1 (Ohio App. 11 Dist. 1982) (unreported decision), *abrogated by Central Trust Co., N.A. v. Jensen,* 67 Ohio St. 3d 140 (1993). Even though the Transamerica case isn't good law anymore, the "semantic gymnastics" turn of phrase is still wonderful—and still used to indicate poor statutory interpretive skills. *See, e.g., Seawall East Townhomes Ass'n, Inc. v. City of Galveston,* 879 S.W.2d 363, 365 (Tex. Ct. App. 1994) ("Moreover, even without semantic gymnastics, the plain meaning of the language gives no indication that the drafters intended to restrict outdoor amusement activities to all those not listed elsewhere in the Zoning Standards. An ordinance or statute should be given a reasonable interpretation to avoid injustice or absurd consequences."); *U.S. v. Mahler,* 442 F.2d 1172, 1175 (9th Cir. 1971) ("The statute fits Mahler's behavior like a glove. It is not for this court, by some sort of semantic gymnastics, to conclude that the Congress did not mean what it has so plainly said.").

- Unless the state permits you to look to the legislature's floor
  debate (some states do not record legislative debate or discussion), don't look to floor debate by the legislature (what
  the intent of the legislators was in passing the legislation) to
  help ascertain the statute's meaning.

Yes, yes; we know that there are a lot of rules that go along with
interpreting statutes. Until you read some statutes yourself, these
rules won't make a lot of sense. (They might not make much sense
after you read some statutes, either.) But both of us love statutes,
and we love trying to figure out what statutes mean. Even though
few statutes are perfectly clear, they're attempts to create logical
systems of regulation.[10]

Here's an example, from §2-207 of the Uniform Commercial Code:

(1) A definite and seasonable expression of acceptance or a writ-
    ten confirmation which[11] is sent within a reasonable time
    operates as an acceptance even though it states terms addi-
    tional to or different from those offered or agreed upon,
    unless acceptance is expressly made conditional on assent
    to the additional or different terms.

(2) The additional terms are to be construed as proposals for
    addition to the contract. Between merchants such terms
    become part of the contract unless:

    (a) the offer expressly limits acceptance to the terms of the
        offer;
    (b) they materially alter it; or
    (c) notification of objection to them has already been given
        or is given within a reasonable time after notice of them
        is received.

(3) Conduct by both parties which[12] recognizes the existence of
    a contract is sufficient to establish a contract for sale although
    the writings of the parties do not otherwise establish a con-
    tract. In such case the terms of the particular contract consist
    of those terms on which the writings of the parties agree,

---

[10] Nancy knows of a classic and fun statutory exercise about banning "vehi-
cles" in parks. *See, e.g., http://www.google.com/search?hl=en&rls=com.microsoft%3
Aen-us&q=no+vehicles+in+parks+exercise&aq=f&oq=&aqi=.*

[11] Nancy hates that the UCC uses "which" instead of "that" here.

[12] Ditto.

together with any supplementary terms incorporated under any other provisions of this Act.

"Between merchants," "seasonable," "contract," and "contract for sale" are all defined terms, so in reading this statute, you'd use the statutory definitions. (Our rule 1.) For the other words, you'd look to the ordinary meanings. (Our rule 2.) As you try to figure out what happened to the "different from" clause in §2-207(1)—it's missing from the rest of the statute—you'd try to apply our rule 3 (read the provisions together, where possible), and you'd certainly want to make a flowchart (our rule 4). This example gets you started, but the art of reading a statute takes a lot of practice.

For our friends who hated statutes but loved case law, the reason was simple: Statutes are dry. There's no plot—no "story." There are no characters for you to love or hate. There are lots of paragraphs, subparagraphs, and sub-subparagraphs. To our friends who preferred cases to statutes we say, "To each his own."

1.4. Highlighting (or How to Increase the Resale Value of Your Used Books)

Some people love the look of pristine (unhighlighted) books. Others mark theirs all to heck. Nancy used to buy her books from upperclass students who had done well in their courses (prehighlighted books) to increase her odds of understanding the material. There are all sorts of methods to highlight books. Some people use different colors for different things: facts of cases, holdings of cases, particular turns of phrase in cases, key facts on which a result in a case turns, definitions in statutes, and so on. Other people just highlight material that seems "important." (Nancy once stuck to highlighting "just the important stuff" in her books until she realized that every page had turned a solid yellow.) We have two recommendations: Experiment to find what works best for you, and buy some erasable highlighters—they let you fix mistakes.

1.5. How to Use Case Briefs

You'll get lots of advice on how to write case briefs, so we want to focus more on how to use them. (We're talking here about using them for class. You might want to review your case briefs before exams, but that's a totally separate topic.) There's no point in briefing cases unless you're using the briefs, and there are only two reasons to use a brief: (1) so that you don't get that deer-in-the-headlights look when the professor calls on you in class to talk about the case;[13] and (2) to figure out how the case adds to your understanding of the rules relating to the topic that you're discussing in class.[14]

Most law students fail to use brief-making as an opportunity to learn the case, preferring instead to copy down quotes from the case into their notes or computers.

These are the things that your brief should help you do:

- Tell you who's suing whom, or who's appealing from what;
- Tell you whether the case is at the trial stage or at an appellate stage;
- Figure out which facts were the most important ones for the court's decision;
- State, *in your own words,* the court's holding and its reasons for its holding; and
- Help you compare this case to cases that you've already discussed in the course.

Realize that some cases are in the textbooks because they're wrongly decided. Don't just assume that every opinion is correct. As Nancy's friend Peter Gurfein once explained, "That's why they call them 'opinions.'"

Ultimately, a brief should help you figure out why, out of all of the cases that the casebook author could have chosen, this particular case is in your book. Maybe it's a good example of a rule or exception; maybe it's a good step-by-step explanation of a principle; or maybe it's just so funny or quirky that the casebook author couldn't resist including it. If you can figure out why the case is in the book, then you're several steps ahead in being able to

---

[13] As Louis Pasteur said, "Chance favors the prepared mind."

[14] You can also use your case briefs for outlining—or at least for preparing to outline.

synthesize the material.[15] Understanding why a case is there means that you *own* that case. It's *yours*. You're *winning*.

1.6. A Typical Week's Study Schedule

Jeff is not sure if his week was or is typical, but this is generally how a typical week of his looked. He was up at the crack of dawn (he's an early bird[16])—thank you, U.S. Marine Corps, for that particular trait—which allowed him to get to school long before the crowd and get a choice location in the library. He preferred to arrive early, as he found it easier to prep for class in the library before most of his classmates were in the building (most students in his class preferred to stay late into the night).

For every hour of classroom instruction that he had, he allocated approximately 1.75 to 2.0 hours for class preparation, outlining, and some study time. A typical semester was 12 to 13 semester classroom hours, which translates to 24 to 26 hours of preparation, outlining, and individual study time during the week (some classes consumed far more time than this schedule—for example, legal research and writing took significantly more time than this schedule indicates). Add in the 12 to 13 hours spent in class, and you've got a pretty full work week in simply preparing for, attending, and outlining and studying for your classes. This schedule did not include study group time,[17] workouts and physical training, or socializing. We've reproduced our best recollection of Jeff's first-year calendar in Appendix A.

Unless they agreed to meet at a different time, Jeff's various study groups met in the late afternoon or early evening and, periodically, on the weekend. As the semester progressed, the time spent in study groups got longer.

---

[15] Many thanks to Nancy's colleague Linda Edwards for emphasizing this point.

[16] So is Nancy, *now* (after 17 years with Jeff).

[17] His study group members were of the opinion that everyone needed to be prepared before showing up for a study group. The group was all in favor of honing skills and knowledge, and it didn't want to waste time in preliminary reviews of materials or in reading anyone's outlines to each other.

Nancy's study schedule was significantly different. She would wake up, eat breakfast, and read every newspaper that she could find—a schedule that continues to this day. Then she would review the readings for the day's classes (which she'd done over the weekend prior to the week's worth of classes). She'd go to class and, immediately after the class that she hated the most, she'd work out. Then she'd shower and either finish out the day's classes or hang out with friends to decompress. If she hadn't done all of the week's readings, she'd work on the readings in the evening. On Saturday mornings, without fail, she'd gather up her week's notes and consolidate them with her briefs and outlines. Her goal was to review each of the prior weeks, add the new week's notes to her consolidated materials, condense that material, and then get rid of[18] the original notes. We've reproduced Nancy's first-year schedule in Appendix B.

The advantage of Nancy's system is that she reviewed every class each weekend, doing her week's reading every Sunday. When finals rolled around, she panicked (because she was a first-year student, and that's what most first-year students do), but she didn't have to try to learn a whole semester's worth of material in a week. While her friends were cramming for finals, she biked downtown and saw a lot of first-run movies.

What if you're not a "keep to a schedule" type of person? Hey, just because both of us are "type A" people,[19] that doesn't mean that you have to keep to a schedule to succeed. But law school requires a lot of reading (hundred-page assignments aren't rare), and you need to find a system that works for you. Make sure to schedule in (uh-oh—there's that word again!) some fun time for yourself. All work and no play only burns you out.

2.   The Secret Way to Learn (Real-Life Examples)

How do you know if you're "getting" law school? The easiest way is to apply what you're learning in everyday life. (Remember

---

[18] Okay, she didn't throw away the notes until after the final exam. But she put them away and didn't look at them again.

[19] See http://en.wikipedia.org/wiki/Type_A_and_Type_B_personality_theory.

everyday life? You had it before you started law school. You read newspapers, watched TV, spoke with friends.) Let's say that you're studying negligence in Torts. While you're waiting for your study group to gather, you flip on the news, and you see that some builder has managed to mess up the rebar for a new building and bits of cement are falling on passers-by. This is very bad news for the passers-by, but it's great news for your study group.[20] You get to talk about duty, cause-in-fact, proximate cause, and damages[21] for the passers-by, should they try to sue the builder.

Or you're sipping coffee and reading the newspaper in the morning. You get ink on your hands from the paper, rub that ink on your pants, and wonder if you have a cause of action against the newspaper publisher for the costs of cleaning your pants. (You don't, but at least you get to work your way through the analysis.)

Want to try the TV version? You could watch NCIS (one of our favorite shows) to figure out whether Gibbs is allowed to head-smack DiNozzo by virtue of DiNozzo's implied consent, whether Abby's use of Caf-Pow creates an implication that her scientific results could be questioned, and so on. Anyway, you get our point. In a few short years, you'll be working your legal magic on real-life situations. You might as well get started now. It'll make those Saturday evening get-togethers with your law school friends a lot more interesting and a lot less whiny.

3.   Preparation Before Class

Jeff's class preparation included not only the designated readings, but also reading from his chosen study guide. (For more on study guides, see Chapter 5.) Unlike Nancy, Jeff preferred to do his preparation immediately before class if at all possible. He also tried to outline that class on the same day as the class itself. When he had back-to-back classes, he accommodated the schedule as needed. His life became a bit more hectic in the second and third years by adding in Law Review, moot court, and clerking at a law firm, in addition to classes, along with class preparation and study time.

---

[20] And people call lawyers "heartless." Go figure.

[21] These four elements are the elements of negligence.

For his night classes[22]—yes, he attended a law school that included a night program—he tried to do his outlining first thing the next morning. Any outlining and reading that didn't get done during the week was allocated to the weekend.

4.   Notetaking During Class

We'll bet that you have a nice laptop, and that you like taking notes on it. Lots of people prefer to take notes on their laptops. Many people, in fact, now type more quickly than they write by hand. But we have two words of caution for you.

First, some professors will forbid the use of laptops during class. No, these professors aren't Luddites. They don't necessarily fear technology. Some of them would just prefer that you listen to them rather than spend your time checking e-mail, updating your Facebook status, IMing your friends, or otherwise distracting your classmates (or yourself) from whatever they're saying at the front of the room.

Second, many professors have noticed that students using laptops have a tendency to take notes as if they were taking dictation in class. These students will write down every single word that the professor says in class, rather than listening to what's going on during class.

We're here to tell you that not every word that comes out of a professor's mouth is earth-shatteringly important.[23] Taking down every single word will not help you learn the material. You have a casebook that has lots and lots of words in it, and—surprise!—not every word in that casebook is of earth-shattering importance, either. Use judgment in taking your notes, whether you're taking them by hand or on your laptop. Otherwise, you're running the age-old risk of "garbage in, garbage out."

---

[22] Jeff took classes from the professors whose teaching styles he liked, especially if they were teaching classes that he wanted to take, for example, Secured Transactions and Negotiable Instruments (e.g., Mike Distelhorst). There were times—because of high demand and limited seating—when the only way to take the classes from those professors was to take night classes.

[23] This point is especially true when the professor is at home with her husband, but it's just as true during class.

Some students take comfort in recording their professors' lectures (don't forget to ask permission first!). If you're an aural learner, then listening to those lectures afterward might help you master the material. For many people, though, listening to the lecture afterward—assuming that you listen to it at all, rather than just accumulate the equivalent of a semester's worth of lectures in a pile of tapes or a series of .mp3 files—is not the most efficient use of your time. A better use of your time would be to make a note of what you don't understand in class, and then go to your professor during office hours to ask questions to clarify what you've missed.

5.   The Postclass "Preparation" Before Outlining

Outlining: No word better evinces the single most important concept in law school during the first few semesters.[24] Several concepts come together under "outlining": creating them, organizing them, distilling them, and studying from them. Right now, the issue is how to prepare for outlining.

First, let's talk about what an outline is and isn't. For Jeff, an outline is a study aid that distills a given course down to its essential concepts. Using this definition, Jeff had more than one draft of an outline for each course. Each draft was progressively more distilled than its predecessor. Ultimately, he condensed each draft until he ended up with one draft that he used for studying for finals—for him, it was little more than a list of black-letter law concepts,[25] coupled with some short examples to give life to the espoused concepts.

---

[24] Actually, Nancy's colleague Jennifer Carr uses a better word: synthesis. And she's absolutely right. But most people use the term outlining, so we're going to go with that one.

[25] "Black-letter law" is a summary of the general rules of a particular law school subject, along with the general exceptions to those rules. In essence, black-letter law is what non-law-trained people think about when they imagine legal education: Someone learns a lot of rules, and those rules apply in virtually every situation. As you know by now, the "rules" for anything are pretty fuzzy, and their application will vary depending on the facts of the case and, occasionally, on policy issues. We're not sure why these rules are called black-letter law, but we have a sneaking suspicion that people use that term because commercial study guides put the rules in boldface.

For Jeff, an outline is *not* simply a compilation of class notes. His class notes were not very legible, nor were they always very understandable, even for him (hence the need to outline quickly after class to try to capture as much information as possible in a comprehensible fashion). If you want to study from your notes instead of with an outline, do yourself a favor and use a separate notebook (or folder in your computer) for each class. That separation will keep things nominally organized—meaning that all the information is in one location—for you. It will make finding what you're looking for much easier. Jeff used separate course notebooks, but crafted a separate outline—separate from the notebooks—because it gave him an opportunity to review his notes while transferring them to the outline. From his perspective, every time that you review your notes, you'll retain a bit more of the material.[26] It's all about getting the information into your brain so that you can remember it and apply it. We'll get much more specific about the sorts of things that you might want to put into your outlines in Chapter 5.

Jeff tried not to delay his outlining by more than a few hours, as he found that the volume of information in some classes made trying to outline on a "weekly" or "biweekly" basis more time-consuming than outlining after every class session. Predictably enough, Nancy was just the opposite. She outlined once a week.

6.   Study Groups Versus Going Solo

Although study groups can make law school considerably easier, you shouldn't feel compelled to participate in one, if a study group won't help you learn the material. The purpose of joining a study group is to help you master the material. A study group that creates synergy—that gives you more than you would have by studying by yourself—is the right group for you. Joining the *wrong*

---

[26] See Nancy's weekly study schedule in Appendix B.

group will be counterproductive; it will make you considerably less efficient. Jeff made such a mistake early in his first semester. Fortunately, he recognized that fact and was smart enough to stop going to that group a week or two later. He studied on his own, and didn't join another study group until the very end of the first semester. He was willing to go it alone partly because he was successful in college studying solo. Additionally, he wanted to be sure that any group that he ultimately joined was going to be one that he actually wanted to join. You don't want to throw yourself into any study group just to be in a group, as it can hurt your performance if the group's methodology does not mesh with your study needs.

6.1. Forming a Study Group

So you've decided to form a study group. How do you go about creating a group that will help you master the material? Sometimes it's as easy as walking up to someone and asking if he wants to study with you. (That's also a tried-and-true method of asking someone out on a date.) But Jeff's school had numerous study rooms lining the exterior and interior walls of the law library. A student could, and sometimes did, simply walk the library looking into the various study rooms for a group of folks that might be able to help him out on a tough subject. Not surprisingly, the "cold call" approach wasn't very successful.

Most people at Jeff's school started studying with the folks that they knew from orientation, the dorm, or class. Although almost all of the various study group memberships tended to evolve over time, some of them stayed intact throughout law school.

Jeff's study group "life" was most successful after he found a core group of fellow students (in his case, three fellow students) who shared similar approaches to study times and patterns. As second- and third-year students, his core study group members took many of the same classes at the same times as he did. Depending on the course, other students joined different subject-matter study groups.

Nancy chose her study group entirely from classmates with whom she enjoyed spending time. Her theory was simple: Find people who were better than she was at some things, so that she could trade her strengths for their strengths.[27] The studying was informal. Her group would get together before some classes and talk over the material. Her group didn't meet regularly, but when it did, people seemed to find that reviewing the material before class helped. Everyone in the group felt less stressed going into a class, having gone over some of the tough cases beforehand. The group kicked into high gear during "dead week," when everyone worked practice exams and then shared practice answers (and way too much coffee) together.

The point of the first two weeks of school is to get yourself into the swing of things. Get the hang of the workload. Find a study schedule that suits you. Find times to work out and decompress. Start to make some friends. Figure out how to brief a case. Don't panic. And, in two more weeks, you can read Chapter 5.

6.2. Study Groups During Finals

Even if you prefer to go solo during the semester, you might find study groups very useful during exam time. Reviewing old exams together will help you find your own blind spots. We'll talk more about this in Chapters 7 and 8.

7.   An Early Warning About People Trying to Psych You Out

As the semester goes along, some people will start talking about how many hours they're studying, how long their outlines are getting, how early they're starting to work on getting summer jobs, and so on. We hope that most of these people are just socially awkward humans who don't know how to have decent conversations with others, because it would be unfortunate to think of these people as sociopaths whose only desire is to turn you into quivering masses of insecurity with low self-esteem. Get our point? Don't let these losers bother you.

---

[27] One of her strengths was keeping a fresh pot of coffee brewing during virtually all waking hours.

CHAPTER FIVE.

The First Month

Nothing concentrates the military mind so much as the discovery that you have walked into an ambush.

—Thomas Packenham, British historian

1.   Finding the Right "Advisors"

As we said before in Chapter 2, you will have all sorts of advice to sift through (including our advice in this book). You'll probably have an upperclass mentor assigned to you, and you've probably met other upperclass students as well. In addition, by now you've gravitated toward some initial friendships with some of your classmates. You might have asked some of your professors for advice, and you might have spoken with your academic support dean. You can also find great advisors in law alumni, other professors, and all sorts of other smart folks in the law school community.[1] How will you sort through all of these differing points of view?

The good news about law school is that it does not *actually* destroy bits of your brain, although you might feel that it has. You came into law school smart; that hasn't changed. You know that you gravitate toward certain ways of learning material (remember our discussion about what type of learner you are, in Chapter 1?). As you sift through advice, then, start by looking for advice that fits with your learning style. Are you a visual learner? Then you might want to think about making some flowcharts. Are you a kinesthetic learner? Then you're going to want to create something new—an

---

[1] Especially in a difficult economy, having more points of view (and more mentors' advice) to sort through can be a very good thing. Your mentors will see the world differently from the way you see it, which will give you more information on which to base your decisions. *See* Elizabeth Garone, *Pile on Mentors in Tough Times,* Wall St. J., Oct. 9, 2009, available at *http://online.wsj.com/article/ SB10001424052748703298004574455172409504420.html.*

outline, a flowchart, flash cards, or all of these—that will force you to do something physical to learn your new skills.

The answer, then, to the question of how to find the right advisors is, in part, to know what kind of advice you need for the type of learner that *you* are.

While we're on the topic of advisors, though, we want to remind you that your non-law-school friends are there to keep you from becoming so self-absorbed that you lose some of what makes you human. They have needs, too, and their needs shouldn't always have to take a back seat to your needs. It's very easy, especially in that first month of law school, to focus on immersing yourself in the study of law to the exclusion of all else: friends, family, eating, sleeping, and so on. For both of us, the first month of law school was a lot like living overseas in a new country. We could figure out the language, with the help of a dictionary, but it took time. We could figure out the customs, through trial and error, but that took time, too. There wasn't anyone holding our hands and walking us through all of the new experiences in the new country. Every single thing we did—making phone calls, buying groceries—was needlessly complex in our new world until we got the hang of how the new country worked. That's why law school can be so all-consuming the first month. And it's okay to be absorbed in it, as long as you remember to break away long enough to get your bearings now and then.

2.   Why Outline Now?

Your professors might have already referred to "making outlines" in some of your classes, and what they're describing is a way of organizing and condensing your notes so that, at the end of the semester, you'll be able to study for finals more efficiently. By the end of your first month, you might not believe that you know enough to begin outlining, but you actually do. By now, you've probably covered some subunits of material in each of your courses. For example, you might have covered what constitutes an offer in your Contracts class. You've read cases about offers and acceptance, and you might have read some Restatements or Uniform Commercial Code sections about offers. You might even have worked some problems in class about offers. And your professor has certainly discussed some hypotheticals about offers during class. Not only do you have enough material about offers, but you actually have too much material. You'll need to condense it, and now's the time. If you outline at the end of every subunit of material, you won't have to panic in those few days between the end of classes and the beginning of the final exam period.

3.   A Better Type of Outline

3.1.   The Garden-Variety Outline, and Why It's Worthless

Most law students "outline" along the following lines, and we'll use "offer" as an example.

I.   Offer

A.   Must be definite. Must create a power of acceptance in the offeree.
B.   *Lucy v. Zehmer.* Selling farm on back of napkin. Joke? Objective manifestation or subjective intent?
C.   *Leonard v. PepsiCo, Inc.* Harrier jet case. Reasonable or joke?
D.   *Lonergan v. Scolnick.* [incessant list of cases continues]

The problem with this outline isn't that it's inaccurate. It's perfectly accurate, if a bit boring. The problem with this outline is that it's, at best, regurgitating everything that the student has learned about offers, without giving the student any help at all in applying what he's learned to any new hypothetical. And being able to apply what you've learned is key.

Law school exams are not about the regurgitation of what you've been told in class, which is very bad news if you're a regurgitation expert. (And many of you were regurgitation experts as undergraduates.) Law school exams are all about taking rules of law, exceptions to those rules, exceptions to the exceptions, and policy considerations, and applying those rules, exceptions, exceptions-to-exceptions, and policies to factual scenarios that you've never seen before. So if you're going to build an outline, for goodness' sake, make it something that you can use in answering law school exam questions.

3.2. A Better Outline

3.2.1. Option 1: An outline as a set of continuums

One way to think about what your law professor is doing in class when she's asking you about a case is that she's trying to locate that case along a continuum, where one end of the continuum represents the perfect application of a rule and the opposite end represents circumstances under which the rule would never apply. So, for an offer, you might think of a continuum this way:

$$\longleftarrow \hspace{8cm} \longrightarrow$$

[**Offer:** a communication that indicates to its recipient a willingness to be bound to the terms that it expresses, and which is specific enough and complete enough that the offeree can manifest acceptance merely by saying "I accept"; the keys to a communication being an offer are DEFINITE AND MATERIAL TERMS that are clear enough that a reasonable offeree would have understood the communication to be an offer and not an invitation to make an offer]

[**NOT an offer:** a communication that's too vague or ambiguous to constitute an offer; one that a reasonable person in the shoes of the offeree would understand to be a joke; one that lacks the DEFINITE AND MATERIAL TERMS necessary to create the ability of the offeree to accept merely by saying "I accept."]

Now that you have a continuum, you could locate cases along that continuum as a way of figuring out which facts might lead a finder of fact to conclude that a communication was more likely to be an offer or more likely not to be an offer. For example, there's a great case[2] involving a kid who saw a Pepsi commercial offering a Harrier fighter jet for 7 million "Pepsi Points." (You can see two of the commercials at issue at *http://www.youtube.com/watch?v=ZdackF2H7Qc* and *http://www.youtube.com/watch?v=Ln0VSA9UJ-w*.) He saved up some points and raised cash to purchase the equivalent of the remainder of the points to get a Harrier, but Pepsi (surprise, surprise) refused to give him the jet.

---

[2] *Leonard v. PepsiCo, Inc.*, 88 F.Supp.2d 116 (S.D.N.Y. 1999), *aff'd*, 210 F.3d 88 (2d Cir. 2000).

Although no court (and, other than Nancy, no law professor of whom she's aware) actively refers to working along a continuum when analyzing a legal issue, in fact, that's what both Mr. Leonard and PepsiCo were doing, right? Leonard was arguing that the commercials put the Harrier squarely on the "offer" side of the continuum, and PepsiCo was arguing that no reasonable person would think that PepsiCo could be offering a Harrier for "Pepsi Points" (in other words, PepsiCo was placing the communication on the opposite side of the continuum). We'll leave it to you to look up where along the continuum the court put the communication. The point is that, for offers, you could organize your class notes and briefs into a series of continuums:[3]

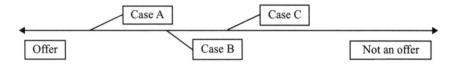

Now, when it's time to answer a hypothetical in class, or to do a practice exam, or even to answer the real exam, you can ask yourself how the new fact situation compares to the cases in your continuum. That's one way to organize the material, and it's far more useful than regurgitating the material that you've already covered with the professor. But that's only one option.

3.2.2.   Option 2: An outline as a set of flowcharts

Another way to help yourself answer a hypothetical (or an exam question) is to create a flowchart that asks you a series of yes—no questions. The idea in parsing your way through a new set of facts is to proceed systematically with an application of a rule (or its exception) to the facts. Law professors don't get that excited if you know a rule, although they get marginally more excited if you're able to state the rule in your own words, rather than reading directly from a case. (After all, if you can't state the rule, you'd be in

---

[3] We make no warranty that this continuum approach will work in all courses, including but not limited to such courses as Constitutional Law. But it's worth a try, isn't it?

big trouble on the exam, wouldn't you?) What gets them excited is your ability to *use* a rule, not merely to identify it.

So here we go with offers again. Let's say that young master Leonard comes to you whining about Pepsi not giving him a Harrier jet when he saved up enough Pepsi Points and raised enough cash to "pay" for one. How might a flowchart on offers help you analyze his problem? The following example can give you a feel for the usefulness of a flowchart.

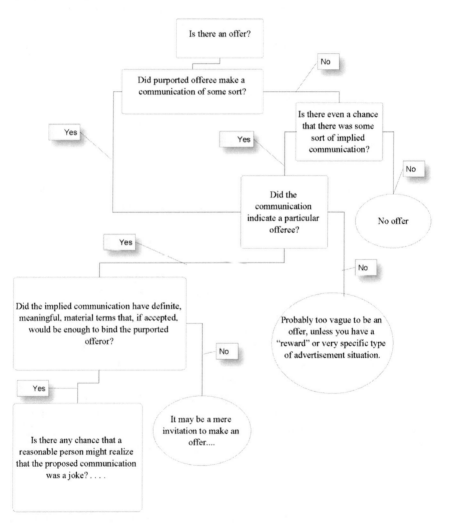

What a flowchart does for you is force you to use the facts of the hypothetical. You're taking the rule (what constitutes an offer) and applying it to specific facts (for example, young master Leonard and his hankering for a Harrier). Both of us, if we used this flow-chart, would have concluded that there was no offer because it was either a garden-variety advertisement ("invitation to make an offer") or, even more likely, it was an obvious joke (Pepsi doesn't have any Harriers to sell). But by using the flowchart, we would have proceeded step-by-step through the rules to the facts, back to the rules, and so on. Again, the step-by-step rules-into-facts-into-analysis process is far more useful to you than simple regurgitation of your notes, unless you're such a kinesthetic learner that you need to rewrite your notes before you can make any sort of outline.

3.2.3. Option 3: An outline as a series of questions

Another way to think of an outline is to think of it as a series of prompts that you have to answer as you proceed, step-by-step, through a set of facts. The point of an outline-as-a-series-of-questions approach is to remind you to search the facts of the hypothetical in front of you for answers to the questions.

Imagine that young master Leonard stalks into your office, slams down the Pepsi Points catalog and a copy of the Pepsi Harrier commercials on your desk, and shouts, "I know that Pepsi owes me a Harrier! I did everything that it asked me to do!" Before you answer him (or have your assistant show him the door), you take out your trusty outline-slash-checklist. Your answers would be the part that we put in italics.

1. A contract requires an offer, acceptance, and consideration to be binding.

   A. Was there an offer?

      i. Did the purported offer make any sort of communication to a specific offeree? *Well, no; not here. Pepsi simply broadcast a couple of commercials and put out a catalog.*

         1) If the answer is no, is there any chance that the purported offer is that rare type of communication to a nonspecific offeree that is either a reward or a

first-come, first-served advertisement for a specific good? *No. Pepsi clearly didn't intend a reward for redeeming points, and it didn't offer "one Pepsi-painted Harrier jet." A reasonable person in the position of an offeree would naturally assume that Pepsi was just trying to drum up business by having people drink Pepsi and collect "frequent drinker" points for doing so. . . .*

3.2.4.   Option 4: Combine all of those other three options, depending on what type of material you're covering

You know where we're heading here. Different types of material will lend themselves to different ways of "outlining." For example, statutes are particularly adaptable to flowcharting. Neither of us is particularly sure what would work in Constitutional Law, although we have a guess that making a historical timeline that indicates who's serving on the Court when particular decisions are handed down might be useful. No matter what method you choose, you want to make sure that you have a way of accessing the rules and exceptions *and* a way of accessing likely issues, for "issue-spotting." Our point is that, until and unless you're going to be a law professor who writes commercial outlines (see Section 5 below), resummarizing material without thinking about how to use it before your exams is a waste of your time. So figure out what methods are going to be the most useful for the type of learner that you are, and get cracking on developing outlines that are tailored to those methods.

3.2.5.   Timelines

Some courses (Constitutional Law comes to mind) really do make more sense when you build timelines of what rules are in place at a given time, when those rules have been reversed, and when the new rules (overruling the old rules) apply. If your professor is interested in policy issues—and most professors are—understanding the timeline for the development of certain rules of law might help you understand how the policy underlying the rules has developed as well. For example, if the law of a subject moved from a strict formalism to something more relaxed, knowing a little about when the law started changing and what was going on in history at that time might help you understand the reasons for the change.

4.   What If You're Going to Have a Multiple-Choice or Closed-Book Exam at the End of the Semester?

The bad news is that neither Jeff nor Nancy is an expert in the psychology of closed-book or multiple-choice exams. (We doubt that most of the law professors who use multiple-choice exams are experts, either.) The good news is that we've both taken these types of exams, in law school and in that lovely hazing ritual called the bar exam. The bar exam involves several days of nothing *but* closed-book and multiple-choice exams.

In many ways, your approach to closed-book exams is going to be exactly the same as your approach to multiple-choice exams. Our advice for closed-book exams is simple. Memorize the rules and exceptions early in the semester—long before your exams will begin. Develop your own study aids and, if you work with a study group, quiz each other on such things as a rule's elements, the exceptions to the rule, and the exceptions to the exceptions. But, as you've already learned, memorization is necessary but not sufficient. You'll have to be able to apply what you're memorizing to the facts in the exam questions. We'll explain how to do that in Chapter 7.

As for multiple-choice exams, the main difference between that type of exam and an essay exam is that a multiple-choice exam lets the professor test more of the course's material in a shorter amount of time. Your studying for a multiple-choice exam will be no different, then, from your studying for an essay exam; how you *take* that exam will be slightly different, and we'll discuss that issue in Chapter 7 as well.[4]

---

[4] Nancy swears by Steve Emanuel's *Strategies and Tactics* books for learning how to take multiple-choice exams.

5.   Commercial Outlines[5]

Your law professors will tell you not to buy them. Your friends have all bought them. There seem to be a million of them. There's *Emanuel's, Gilbert's, Nutshells,* and countless other summaries and explanations of various law school courses—all of them written by very smart people, all of them designed to help you through understanding what you're reading outside class and discussing in class.

We have no real beef against using these extra study aids, as long as you don't use them instead of your assigned readings and instead of making your own outlines. Heck, Nancy could not have survived Property or Federal Income Tax without her study aids. But take what those study aids say with a grain of salt. Unless your professor has written your particular study aid, your professor's take on the course outranks whatever your study aid says about it.

As for commercial case briefs ("canned briefs"), we *suppose* that there might be a circumstance where someone else's reading and briefing of a case might help you in class or in preparing for your final exam, if you're particularly time-pressured, but frankly, we think that you'd be better off book-briefing the cases,[6] or even trading briefs with some of your friends in the class. At least that way, you'd be preparing the briefs in the manner most likely to help you when your professor calls on you.[7]

6.   Hornbooks

Hornbooks are mini-treatises[8] written by law professors who have spent years and years thinking about particular subject areas.

---

[5] There are other types of study aids, such as flash cards, law summaries, DVDs, and the like. Your learning style should guide you in your selection of the best study aids for you. All we ask is that you use study aids to, well, *aid* your studying, not to replace it entirely.

[6] "Book-briefing" is where you brief the case directly into your casebook. You color-code the facts of the case in one highlighter color; then you color-code the issues in a different highlighter color, the holding in yet another color, and the reasoning in still another color. Our advice? Read the case a few times first. Highlighters are difficult to erase, unless you buy the newfangled erasable kind.

[7] Apologies to any of Nancy's colleagues who write any canned briefs.

[8] Yep, treatises are large hornbooks. Many times, they're multi-volume hornbooks.

There are several different hornbooks for each first-year (and upperclass) course, and the beauty of these is that each of them is well thought-out. When Nancy was a confused first-year law student, she started with hornbooks to straighten out her confusion when she was making outlines. Her order of preparing outlines was as follows:

- Go to notes.
- Do first draft of outline.
- Figure out what parts were "fuzzy."
- Read hornbook to see if that helped.
- Read commercial outline to see if *that* helped.
- Redo draft of outline.

7. Test-Drive Your Outline

To make sure that you're on track after your first month of law school, try this trick: Get together with a small group of friends. Ask each friend to make up a hypothetical based on an area that you've already covered in class and that each of you has already outlined. Exchange hypotheticals and try to answer them, using your own outlines. The easiest way to test whether your outline is going to help you is to practice using it. If your outline's not helpful, change it based on what would make it more helpful to you. (Don't look now, but you've just created a study group.)

8. Student Organizations: Join Now or Wait?

By now, you've gotten more used to law school: Your studying's in a nice groove, you have a circle of friends, and you're used to feeling a bit lost (but you're not quite as panic-stricken by the feeling). Student organizations are putting signs up all over school, and you're wondering if you should join any of them now. Here's one way to look at the issue, and we apologize in advance if we sound a tad calculating: Your primary job in law school is to learn.

Every minute that you take away from your primary job should be a minute that's worthwhile to you. If you take some time away from your primary job to reduce your stress (perhaps by working out, seeking some quiet time, or hanging out with friends) or nurture those close to you, great. Reducing stress and maintaining your personal ties is important.

With this advice in mind, as you sort through the various student organizations, ask yourself if each organization that interests you will help with your primary job (for example, organizations that help their members study, that help you with career prospects, such as organizations that help their members network with practicing lawyers, or that help you relax for a while so that you can return, refreshed, to your primary job, like a sports club). Every school has various affinity clubs: clubs for people who share common interests. There are clubs for people who are interested in real estate law or public interest law, clubs for people who share the same religion or ethnicity, and clubs for older students. You might choose to join one or more organizations or to give all organizations a pass until your second year (or never). But whatever you do, don't forget that your primary job is to learn. Period.

9.   Congratulations! You've Made It Through Your First Month of Law School!

Do you still have friends and family? No unusual tics? Then you're doing fine.

CHAPTER SIX.

Some Advice About Writing

More has been screwed up on the battlefield and misunderstood in the Pentagon because of a lack of understanding of the English language than any other single factor.

—Gen. John W. Vessey, Jr.

By the time you hit your second semester, you've become a value-maximizing law student. You're more efficient (already). You not only read cases and statutes more quickly, but you also take notes more quickly, and you're following class discussions better. That's the good news. You actually *have* come a long way.

The bad news is that you may be tempted to do some arithmetic, add up the credit hours assigned to the casebook-based courses (e.g., Contracts, Civil Procedure, Constitutional Law), look at the credit hours assigned to your Legal Research and Writing course, and decide to make the value-maximizing decision to devote less time to this "non-casebook-based course." That decision is, as we like to say, A Huge Mistake.

Yes, the readings for your casebook-based courses take a lot of time, and the professors who teach those courses will be extremely frustrated with you if you show up unprepared. (Remember, though, that we just said that you're more efficient in your second semester.) But lawyers *must* do two things, no matter the field:

1. Think.
2. Communicate.

Your writing course teaches you how to do both of these things—and you can't communicate well without first doing a good job of thinking. And, unfortunately for clients, many lawyers neither think well nor communicate well. For better or for worse, throughout your entire career, your bosses, your clients, and your colleagues will judge your abilities and your intelligence by your thinking and communication skills. Excel at these two skills, and you'll have a real edge. (Of course, that's easier said than done.)

1.   You Can Become a Better Writer (and Thinker) in Law School

Twice a year (at grading time), Nancy bemoans the writing ability of her students. She's joined by every law professor at every law school, from the best schools in the country to the ones that are further down the pecking order. Some of her students do write well. But many write poorly, and poor writing distresses Nancy greatly.[1] Not only does she see a lack of basic writing skills, she sees a lack of organization in the written product: the failure to use thesis sentences, outlines,[2] and a logical progression of arguments.

Although poor writing can indicate a lack of understanding about the subject matter or a failure to organize material coherently, poor writing does not always indicate a poor grasp of the underlying material. But why give someone the impression that you don't understand what you're trying to say? The profession of law has, traditionally, been a profession of talented and passionate writers. Clients deserve—and need—lawyers who write better than the average person writes.

1.1.   What If You've Entered Law School Without Already Knowing the Basic Rules of Grammar?

There are some undergraduate degrees that don't require significant writing projects. According to Jeff, Criminal Justice is one of these degrees,[3] and he admits that he was woefully underskilled as a writer when he entered law school. Therefore, it's possible to enter law school without knowing the basic rules of grammar. But there's no excuse for continuing in ignorance. There are two basic books that can help you learn the rules. Try William Strunk, Jr. & E.B. White, *The Elements of Style* (4th ed. 1999) or Lynne Truss, *Eats,*

---

[1] Jeff has actually seen Nancy send letters to the *Wall Street Journal* and the *New York Times* when she is particularly frustrated by poor writing in advertisements or news stories.

[2] The type of outlines that you used—or were supposed to use—before you entered law school.

[3] Before you Criminal Justice majors out there get all huffy, take another look at Jeff's bio.

Shoots & Leaves: The Zero Tolerance Approach to Punctuation (2006). (The latter book is based on British grammar, but it's very funny and has some memorable examples.) You can even try *The Chicago Manual of Style* (15th ed. 2003).

Perhaps you're a member of the texting generation, and you believe—as one person did, in response to one of Nancy's blog posts[4]—that it's more important what you say than how you say it:

> Legally UnBound said . . .
> I love it when a [b]log sparks a FIRE. Ms. Rapoport, you may be right, but you are wrong. This has always been an issue, from generation to generation. Yes, you are showing your, er, uh, "experience[.]" What you are encountering is linguistical evolution in the American lexicon/grammar, not just "those lazy kids." It's just how it is. I don't like it, but it is. The up and coming generation has to deal with the changes that technology creates in language, the increased acceptance of other cultures and languages in society, the increased internationalization of our language . . . not that it wasn't already. Don't worry[;] the foreign speakers will catch up to our "lazy" evolving ways, too. They always have.
> . . . .
> So the question is[:] are we devolving or evolving?
> The most relevant comment is that "grammar can be esoteric." Great, someone said it!! Even though that comment is like "nails on a chalkboard" to many, it is true. In the end, it really should be more about "what" we are saying, instead of digressing to "how" it is being said. Much ado about nothing.

Nope. We don't buy that argument for one second. Surgeons without scalpels aren't supposed to dig into someone's body with putty knives. Plumbers without wrenches aren't supposed to use twist-ties to fix clogged drains. And you're not supposed to represent clients without the full panoply of good communication skills. If you don't know the difference between "it's" and "its," learn the difference.[5]

---

[4] *http://nancyrapoport.blogspot.com/2009/06/i-fear-for-next-generation-of-lawyers.html*. Yes, Nancy wrote this post shortly after she turned her semester's grades in, and no, she's not sorry that she wrote the post.

[5] And if you think that there is actually a word called "its'," then you need to read several more books about writing.

We aren't going to make you feel bad about coming to law school without this knowledge, but we intend to make you feel awful about attempting to survive the first year of law school without acquiring it. For a list of other rules that you should learn, see Section 3 (Nancy's pet peeves).

1.2. You Can't Trust Computers to Do Your Dirty Work for You

Many of you have tried to breathe a sigh of relief when finishing papers by clicking "spell check" and "grammar check," and then accepting all of the recommendations. Well, computers are useful but certainly aren't 100 percent reliable.[6] If you don't know the rules yourself, then you won't know when the computer's making a mistake.

Don't believe us? What about all of those stories about billing mistakes, like the person who received a $218 trillion phone bill?[7] Face it: Computers are programmed by humans, and humans make errors. That means that the spell-check and grammar-check programs have errors, too. There's just no excuse for not knowing the basic rules. And if you want to be a great lawyer, then you need to learn the advanced rules as well.

For lawyers, the written word matters. The best lawyers will take time to choose the exact word(s) that they need. They'll consult both a dictionary and a thesaurus. They'll read sentences aloud to see if they flow well. They'll shorten sentences to make sure that the

---

[6] Think "Hal" in 2001: A Space Odyssey (MGM 1968).

[7] Associated Press, *Think your phone bill is high? Try $218 trillion, Malaysian man hit with gigantic bill, ordered to pay up or face prosecution,* April 9, 2006 (*http://www.msnbc.msn.com/id/12247590/*).

sentences are clear. (One of Jeff's pet peeves is using a 40-word sentence when a 10-word sentence would be clearer and more persuasive.) (We edited these chapters several times, and we *know* that we could have edited them even more.) If we wanted to beat a dead horse here, and we do, our lesson is edit, edit, edit—and then edit some more.

In sum, the best lawyers take pride in their written work. But more important than taking pride in your own work is the professional edge that good work product will give you. For example, the vast majority of courts will decide their cases based on the quality of the arguments that are made before them in written motions, complaints, and briefs. The same is true not only for litigation, but also for transactional documents. Every client will both judge your abilities and rely on your expertise on the basis of the quality of your written product. We want you to be among the best lawyers. Start taking pride in your written product now.

2. There Is No Worse Crime in Academia Than Plagiarism

We've been shocked at how many law students have been caught plagiarizing and have pleaded that they didn't even realize that they *were* plagiarizing. Each of these students will have to face the state bar's scrutiny when he applies to sit for the bar exam. The bar examiners will ask lots of questions and put the applicant through plenty of turmoil while the examiners try to figure out why the applicant didn't act within the ethical boundaries when he was in school. Simply stated, plagiarism, just like other forms of cheating in school, *matters;* don't do it. Here's an easy check:

1. Did you come up with whatever you've written all by yourself (the idea or the phrase)?
2. If the answer is yes, then the idea or phrase is yours.
3. If the answer is no, then you need to give credit to the person whose idea or phrase you're using.
4. And if you're using someone's exact words, then you need to put quotation marks around those words or—if you're

using a block quote[8]—otherwise indicate that you didn't write those words yourself.

As much as we'd have hoped that everyone in law school would have learned the rules of attribution of ideas in grammar school or at least during college, apparently, we're wrong. Perhaps, students are so accustomed to doing computer-based research that they're copying and pasting their research into files and not clearly marking when the files involve someone else's ideas. (Our cure for this: Put the other person's words in YELLOW HIGHLIGHTING OR IN A LARGER AND DIFFERENT FONT. See? We just put this phrase in a different font, and you saw the difference easily. It's hard to mistake yellow highlighted text for your own work if you use yellow highlighting to indicate *someone else's* work.[9])

The best description of what constitutes plagiarism that we've found is set forth in the University of Tennessee-Knoxville's *Writing Standards in Law School,* available at *http://www.law.utk.edu/ administration/records/writing-standards.shtml.* You can save yourself a lot of heartache by taking a look at this well-written document.

Oh, and by the way, most schools have software that helps professors root out plagiarism. Plagiarists can run, but they can't hide.

3.   Nancy's Pet Peeves

3.1. *Passive Voice[10]*

Law, more than any other discipline, craves assigning blame to someone. In real life, people do things to objects (or other people). Don't say, "The cat was thrown off the bed by Jeff." Say, "Jeff threw the cat off the bed."[11]

---

[8] Check your Bluebook or ALWD book for the rules on block quotes.

[9] Nancy uses the yellow highlighter technique every time she does research for a new article, and it saves her a great deal of time.

[10] Passive voice is one of Jeff's all-time biggest pet peeves, too.

[11] Other examples of active voice include:

- The cat tripped Jeff while he was walking down the stairs.
- The cat woke Jeff up extremely early to take revenge for being thrown off the bed.

3.2.   Unclear References

Instead of saying "this will," identify the "this" to which you're referring. Richard Nixon was famous for (among other things) saying, "Let me say this about that." Talk about unclear references!

3.3.   Don't Use "Impact" Unless You're Discussing a Collision

Most people don't mind it if you use "impact" to mean "affect." Nancy, however, believes that to impact means to touch physically, and she believes that most people who use the word "impact" probably mean either "effect" (as in "this interpretation will have an effect on . . .") or to "affect" (as in "this interpretation will affect the firm . . .").

3.4.   Know the Difference Between "That" and "Which"

"That" is a "pointing to" word (e.g., "Go sit in the chair that is in the corner."). "Which" introduces a clause that isn't the main part of a sentence. Use "which" by introducing it with a comma. (A comma doesn't precede "that.") So, in the sentence, "The chair, which is in the corner, is brown," if you'd set the clause aside with parentheticals, use "which." If you don't need the clause, you probably should either eliminate it or use "which" to begin the clause. (Don't forget the comma again at the end of the clause, if your sentence continues beyond the clause.)

3.5.   Avoid Lawyerese and Wordiness or Redundancy

An example of this mistake would be using "at a future point in time" instead of "later" or "in the future." Lawyers do not charge by the word, even though some of them think that they do. Nor do they charge by the pound, although we're sure that they wish that they could. Lawyerese is one of Jeff's pet peeves, too.

• The cat climbed back on the bed no matter how many times Jeff threw her off of it. *See also http://www.youtube.com/watch?v=bETCusT5kNM.*

3.6.   Subject–Verb Disagreement and Noun–Pronoun Disagreement

If "client" is singular, then the verb following the client is also singular. If "client" is singular, then you can use "his," "her," or "its," as the case may be. You shouldn't use "they" after a singular noun. Take the time to proofread.

3.7.   Misused Temporal Words

Many of you use temporal words improperly. Here's a translation for you:

The word that you *think* that you want to use	What that word *really* means	Use *this* word instead	Try remembering this sentence
While	Simultaneously	Although or though	Juggling knives *while* riding a unicycle is challenging, *although* experienced street performers can do it.
Since	After the other thing I mentioned	Because or as—to imply a cause-and-effect relationship	*Because* it's been a long time *since* I was a child, I can't quite remember my childhood nightmares.

3.8. *You Cannot Make a Singular Noun Plural by Adding an Apostrophe and an "s," No Matter How Many Times You Try*

The "plural with apostrophe and s" sin is Nancy's biggest pet peeve. *See* Lynne Truss, *Eats, Shoots & Leaves: The Zero Tolerance Approach to Punctuation* (2004). And as for confusing "it's" and "its"—a confusion that gives Nancy nervous tics—try this trick: Search your paper for "it's." Every time "it's" appears, read the sentence aloud to see if you mean "it is." If you don't mean "it is," then you shouldn't use "it's" there.

3.9. *Misspelling Names*

On the subject of proofreading, please spell your professor's name correctly on all papers. They all get touchy about the misspelling of their names, even if they won't mention that issue to you.

CHAPTER SEVEN_____

Preparing for Exams

Anybody who doesn't have fear is an idiot. It's just that you must make the fear work for you. Hell, when somebody shot at me, it made me madder than hell, and all I wanted to do was shoot back.
—Gen. Robin Olds, U.S. Air Force

1. "Drill the Skills": Using Hypotheticals and Old Exams

For the vast majority of you, your entire semester has led up to this: taking exams. You've gone to class, done your outlines, studied hard, and (perhaps) formed study groups. Now it's time to show what you've learned on your exams.

We view law school exam-taking as a sport. As with any other sport, the best way to perform is to drill the skills that form the foundation and component parts of the sport. If you're a golfer, you'd go to the driving range and also practice chipping, bunker shots, and putting. If you're a ballroom dancer—and it is *too* a sport!—you'd practice forward and backward walks, arm styling, and lead/follow. Exam-taking is a sport as well, and you have all of the necessary tools to practice it.

If your school has either practice or real exams on file, grab every exam on file for each of the subjects on which you'll be tested during your first semester. It doesn't matter if your professor wrote those exams or not, although naturally that professor's exams will be your top priority.[1] Get them all. If your school doesn't have any practice exams on file, get your hands on other schools' exams[2] and on study guides with practice exams. Then lay out a schedule that

_____

[1] Just as in college, you're taking the professor's course, not just an abstract nameless, faceless course. Therefore, writing the exam with that professor as your audience is going to be very important.
[2] You have friends at other law schools or access to Google, right?

93

involves reviewing your outlines and taking practice exams. That's step one.[3]

2.   Working With Classmates

Step two will involve setting time aside to meet with your study group, or a selected group of classmates if you don't have a study group, to go over your answers and strategies to taking these practice exams. If you work with a group of classmates, you'll soon realize that you have blind spots (meaning that you didn't see every issue that might have been in the question), and so do they. You might systematically miss particular issues that others will find. By going over a series of exams with your classmates, you'll learn to create a checklist of things that you typically miss.

A side benefit of going over practice exams with your classmates is that misery loves company. Moreover, the more questions that you do, the more likely that you're likely to recognize similar questions or issues on future exams.

3.   The Nitty-Gritty: How to Take a Law School Exam

3.1.   Types of Law School Exams

There are all sorts of law school exams. Some professors give multiple-choice or short-answer essay exams. Some (very, very few) give oral exams, in which a student walks into the exam room and the professor asks him a series of questions to determine the student's understanding of the materials. Most professors give essay exams. In an essay exam, you're presented with hypothetical

---

[3] If you have very trustworthy upperclass friends with good outlines from the professors who are teaching your courses, or if you have access to a reliable "outline bank," then you can use those outlines as backups for your own outlines. But you know we're going to emphasize that the outline you make is always, always going to be better than anyone else's outline, simply because you've put your own work into it. The simple act of making your outline will help you to learn the material.

fact situations, and you need to write essays that answer how the hypotheticals would likely turn out from a legal standpoint.

Even those essay exams can vary. Some essays can be single-topic, short-answer questions, whereas others can go on for pages (often called "issue-spotter" exams.) Some essay exams are given in class (in a classroom setting), so that a four-credit-hour course might have a four-hour exam associated with it. Other exams are take-home tests, so that the professor might give her students more than the traditional amount of time to answer the exam questions. Some exams are open-book, which lets students look up material before answering the questions; others are closed-book, meaning that students are not allowed to bring any notes or other materials into the exam room. Finally, some are combinations of all of the above. For example, Nancy gives her students take-home, open-book essay exams. Jeff had a Negotiable Instruments professor who gave in-class exams that were a combination of short-answer and essay exams.

Is your head spinning with options yet? The good news is that your preparation for the essay exams will be roughly the same, whether the exam is in-class or take-home, open-book or closed-book, issue-spotter or short-answer. The bad news is that although some professors give multiple-choice exams, neither of us is particularly confident about giving you advice on how to prepare for multiple-choice exams. We'll give you some advice about taking multiple-choice exams in this chapter, along with plenty of advice on how to take essay exams.

3.2. The Point of an Essay Exam

The point of a law school exam is to not only test your mastery of the material, but also to separate the students who simply understand the basics of the course (or who didn't even "get" the basics) from those who have truly mastered the course's concepts. There are four possible options, using the traditional and ubiquitous IRAC method, for demonstrating your prowess, but only one of these will actually work.

3.2.1. What on Earth is IRAC?

IRAC stands for Issue, Rule, Application, and Conclusion. It's a way of organizing your exam answer to make sure that you've efficiently covered everything that your professor will be looking for when she's grading your exam.

- *Issue.* What tricky problem does the hypothetical in the exam raise? (For example, is there a contract between A and B?) There are usually several issues in a long hypothetical. (For example, if there's a contract, and if it's been breached, then what are A's remedies vis-à-vis B? If the contract hasn't been breached, is A liable to B in any other way?)
- *Rule.* What legal rule(s) applies to the issue? There will be at least one applicable rule (or exception) per issue.
- *Application.* Using the facts stated in the hypothetical, as well as any fair inferences that you can draw from those facts, how would the legal rules that you've identified resolve the issues that you've identified?
- *Conclusion.* Not surprisingly, after you've spent a few paragraphs on analysis that begins "on the one hand," moves smoothly to "on the other hand," and somehow finds a *third* hand, at some point, your answer needs to "call the ball."[4]

3.2.2.   Of the four elements of IRAC, which one counts the most?

We don't want to speak for all of your professors, but if we were betting people, we would put our money on the application element. Here's why. By the time that you get to finals, most of your colleagues will be able to state most of the legal rules (the "black-letter law") that you covered in your courses with some degree of accuracy. So your professors won't be able to compare you on the "rules" part of IRAC. There will be parts of the questions on which reasonable people can disagree, so the "conclusions" part of IRAC won't garner you many points, either. As between "issues" and

---

[4] When aviators "call the ball," they are "sight[ing] the red fresnel light that shows a pilot to be on the correct approach path." *http://en.wiktionary.org/wiki/call_the_ball.* When we say "call the ball," we mean that you should be indicating that you are on your way to making a conclusion among all of the alternative interpretations that the facts of the hypothetical have presented to you.

"application," chances are good that many of your classmates will be able to find many of the issues hidden in the exam hypotheticals, too. What does that leave? Exactly. You will demonstrate your superior understanding of the material with your analysis: your application of the legal rules to the facts to resolve the issues raised by the hypotheticals.

Stated simply, you will garner the most points on your exams by

> **APPLYING**
> the **LEGAL RULES**
> to the **FACTS** in the exam hypotheticals
> to resolve the **ISSUES** raised by those hypotheticals.

3.3. How to Analyze an Exam Hypothetical

Most exam hypotheticals are loaded with issues that are, in turn, chock full of ambiguities. Here's why: If a professor gives you an issue with a clear answer, there's nothing to discuss and, therefore, nothing for you to use to demonstrate your superior grasp of the material. So the professor needs to give you lots of ambiguous issues—and you need to be able to figure out where, in the continuum of rule and exception, the facts in the hypothetical lie.

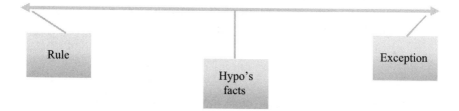

A well-written exam will have several issues smack-dab[5] in the middle of various continuums,[6] so that you'll be able to say, "On the one hand, it could be *this,* but on the other hand, it could be *that.*" Generally, it's how you interpret certain facts that will swing the decision from one side of the continuum to the other. A well-reasoned answer will explain which facts are the critical

---

[5] Yes, Nancy is from Texas, and she really does say things like "smack-dab."
[6] Okay, the plural of continuum is continua, but that just looks pretentious to us.

facts and how varying spins on that fact could drive a different result.[7]

3.3.1. An example of a well-written question: Paul Bateman's burglary hypothetical

In 1999, Nancy discovered this hypothetical, which was drafted by SCALE[8] faculty at Southwestern University's School of Law in the early 1980s. The hypothetical is used frequently by Professor Paul Bateman in Southwestern's Academic Support Program, and Nancy has fallen in love with it.[9] We will refer to the hypothetical throughout as Professor Bateman's hypothetical.

Burglary: "the breaking and entering of a dwelling of another in the nighttime with intent to commit a felony therein."

One night, when it was raining lightly, Dan went looking for Vic, saying "I'll get that guy for cheating me out of $100." Dan took a loaded pistol with him. Not knowing where Vic lived, Dan wandered around the city for several hours. Suddenly, it began to rain heavily. Dan smashed a window in the very first house he saw, and entered. He remained inside the house until the rain stopped. As Dan was about to leave, Vic came in the front door. Startled, Dan pulled out his gun and fired one shot, missing Vic. Dan then ran out the door. As it turned out, Dan had broken into Vic's house; Dan did not know whose house it was when he broke in. Dan has been charged with burglary.

What result?

---

[7] For example, virtually everyone in your class should be able to state that a contract can only be formed if there's an offer, an acceptance, and consideration. Most, but not all, of the students in your class might be able to tease out the difference between a joke offer and a real offer. Still fewer might be able to tease out the difference between a joke offer in one culture and an offer that would be serious in another culture. After all, the test for whether a purported offer is a joke or not will depend on what group of "reasonable people" the lawyers choose: reasonable people in the offeror's culture, or reasonable people in the offeree's culture.

[8] "SCALE" stands for Southwestern's Conceptual Approach to Legal Education. *See http://www.swlaw.edu/academics/jd/scale.*

[9] Many thanks to Professor Bateman and his colleagues at Southwestern for letting us use this hypothetical in our book.

Law professors love to write "What result?" as the "question" part of their exams. It's vague and gives you no way to structure your answer. In a way, it's a microcosm of the first semester of law school: all style, no guidance. Not to worry. We're here to help.

3.3.2.   One way to think about Professor Bateman's hypothetical

When Nancy teaches her students how to answer law school exam questions, she first gives them Professor Bateman's hypothetical and walks them through the various issues in the question. Then she hands out the following mock stream-of-consciousness "welcome to Nancy's brain as a first-year law student" narrative. You can see that mock narrative in Appendix D.

Here's one way to outline the answer. Start by listing the elements of the rule: burglary is (1) the breaking and (2) entering (3) of a dwelling (4) of another (5) in the nighttime (6) with intent to commit a felony (7) therein.

Element	Facts in hypothetical supporting or eliminating element	Conclusion re: element
The breaking	Dan smashed (broke) the window	"Breaking" established.
and entering	Dan entered the house	"Entering" established.
of a dwelling	A dwelling is a place in which people live. Houses are dwellings. Dan broke into a house.	We can presume that the house is a dwelling, so this element is established.
of another	This is not *Dan's* house.	"Of another" established.
in the nighttime	Hypo starts out with "One night." But, Dan walked around for "several" hours, and	We might have a problem here. If we guess that, by the time he broke into the house,

Element	Facts in hypothetical supporting or eliminating element	Conclusion re: element
	he stayed in the house until the rain stopped. It's not clear that he was there very long, but we can certainly infer that he was only there a matter of minutes or hours, rather than days.	it wasn't at night, that solves the problem— you can't have a burglary during the day. But the professor will not want to make it that easy. We'll have to hedge our bet.
with intent to commit a felony	Well, he was packing a gun, he was angry and looking for Dan, and he did fire the firearm. But he entered the house only after it began to rain, and he started to leave after the rain stopped. At the time that he entered the house, he didn't know that it was Vic's house. On the *other* other hand, who breaks into a house to get out of the rain? [Affirmative defense of private necessity: He had a disease and was going to melt like the Wicked Witch of the West if he didn't get in out of the rain. He had no intent to commit any crime . . . ☺]	This one's tough, too. Another time to hedge our bet.

Element	Facts in hypothetical supporting or eliminating element	Conclusion re: element
therein	He shot at Vic in the house. Shooting at someone is probably a felony under these circumstances (We're glad we don't have to analyze that here!), but did Dan have intent to commit *that* felony, or any other felony, while he was inside the house? And did he have that intent when he *entered* the house?	Did Dan intend to commit a felony *in this particular house* or simply *against Vic*? Another hedge here.
Conclusion		Tough call, but Dan might possibly be acquitted of burglary: (1) The incident might not have happened at night; and (2) the prosecution might not be able to prove that Dan intended to commit a felony while inside this house because of the "rain" thing and because Dan didn't even know it was Vic's house. Isn't there some "burden of proof" thing that we can use as a tie-breaker here?

The advantage of this sort of grid outline is that it forces you to link each element of the legal rule with specific parts of the facts in the hypothetical.

3.3.3. Another way to view Professor Bateman's hypothetical: the Beazley approach

When she was a novice law professor at The Ohio State University College of Law,[10] Nancy was lucky enough to have a senior colleague, Professor Mary Beth Beazley, who taught Nancy a lot about teaching. Professor Beazley also wrote a wonderful article, *The Self-Graded Draft: Teaching Students to Revise Using Guided Self-Critique*,[11] which demonstrated how students could separate their use of legal rules from their use of facts:

> For example, most legal writers agree that when applying law to facts, the writer should repeat the "key words" of the rule—i.e., the words or phrases that are in controversy in the current case. In my courses, I refer to the "key words" as the "phrase that pays," and I tell my students that when they apply law to facts, they should expect to write a sentence that translates approximately as "phrase that pays [equals or does not equal] legally significant facts." Thus, two "agreed-upon requirements" are 1) phrase that pays and 2) legally significant facts. Coincidentally (this coincidence does not always occur, but it often does), these agreed-upon requirements are also "markers" that identify a good example of application of law to facts. Accordingly, to help identify strong application of law to facts, the self-grading guidelines ask the student to highlight the phrase that pays in one color and legally significant facts in another color.
>
> When using this method, the writer can graphically see where he or she talked about the rule language and the facts by reviewing the colors alone. If the two colors are never found close together, the writer can scrutinize the entire section to see if 1) the writer failed to apply the law to the facts, or 2) the writer applied the law to the facts, but did so ineffectively, either by using synonyms instead of the phrase-that-pays, or by completing the application in a conclusory way instead of referring to specific facts. If the two colors do appear close together, the writer

---

[10] Yes, "The" is part of Ohio State's name, and now the school is called the Moritz College of Law.

[11] Mary Beth Beazley, *The Self-Graded Draft: Teaching Students to Revise Using Guided Self-Critique*, 3 J. Legal Writing Inst. 175 (1997); *see also* Mary Beth Beazley, *A Practical Guide to Appellate Advocacy* (2002).

can scrutinize those particular sentences to make sure that the intersection between law and facts is clearly explained.

When a reliable marker can be found, self-grading guidelines can also help reveal other weaknesses in legal writing. For example, many legal writers agree that the major discussion of how a rule applies to a set of facts should occur only after the writer has identified and appropriately explained the rule. Unfortunately, however, many legal writers mistakenly—and almost always ineffectively—launch into a long factual discussion/application immediately after the introductory paragraph. After they discuss the facts, they articulate and explain the rule, and then they explain the facts again when they apply the rule to the facts.

Completing a self-grading exercise can help writers to realize when they have applied the rule to the facts before articulating the rule. In the exercise, the writer is asked to highlight all client facts in green and the phrase-that-pays in pink, wherever either appears. If the writer has discussed facts in too much detail too soon, he or she will find large chunks of green highlighting before the numerous pink highlights that indicate identification and explanation of the legal rule. This graphic signal lets the writer know that he or she needs to scrutinize that "chunk of green" to make sure that the application of the rule has not preceded its explanation.[12]

Professor Beazley's advice is extremely useful in every type of writing. Let's apply it to Professor Bateman's hypothetical, using it, first, to highlight legal rules and relevant facts.[13] To make it easier on our publisher, we've used different boldface and italics rather than using different colors, but you get the idea.

Burglary: "the BREAKING and ENTERING of a DWELLING of ANOTHER in the NIGHTTIME with INTENT TO COMMIT A FELONY THEREIN."

One **night,** when it was **raining lightly, Dan went looking for Vic,** saying **"I'll get that guy for cheating me out of $100." Dan took a loaded pistol with him. Not knowing where Vic lived, Dan wandered around** the city for **several hours. Suddenly,** it **began to rain heavily. Dan smashed a window** in the **very first house he saw,** and **entered. He remained inside the**

---

[12] *Id.* at 182-184 (footnotes omitted).

[13] The italics highlight the components of the legal rule, and the bold type highlights the relevant facts.

**house until the rain stopped. As Dan was about to leave, Vic
came in the front door. Startled,** Dan **pulled out his gun and
fired one shot, missing Vic. Dan then ran out the door.** As it
turned out, **Dan had broken into Vic's house; Dan did not know
whose house it was when he broke in.** Dan has been charged
with burglary.

Your mission, should you choose to accept it[14] (cue the *Mission:
Impossible* music)[15] is to take all of the facts and figure out how they
relate to all of the legally relevant "phrases that pay." The secret to
making sure that you squeeze every possible point out of every exam
hypothetical is to make sure that you have used every relevant fact (all
of the boldfaced terms) and linked it with at least one of the highlighted
rule-element phrases. Nancy recommends that you use different-
colored highlighters or other ways of making notations on the exam
hypotheticals themselves so that you don't miss any relevant facts.

Here's one way to write an answer to Professor Bateman's
hypothetical. There are a lot of good ways to write such an answer,
so don't fret if your answer doesn't look like this one.[16]

To charge Dan with burglary, the prosecutor would have to
prove, beyond a reasonable doubt, that Dan had (1) broken and
(2) entered (3) the dwelling (4) of another (5) in the nighttime
(6) with intent to commit a felony therein. The prosecutor will
have difficulty proving all of these elements beyond a reasonable
doubt, although some of them are "givens."

The hypothetical itself states that Dan "smashed a window"
(broken) in "the very first house he saw" (the house would be a
dwelling of another, in that it wasn't Dan's own house), and that
Dan "entered" the house (thereby establishing "entering"). So far,
so good.

But the prosecutor won't have such an easy job proving the
remaining elements of burglary. Although the hypothetical starts

---

[14] And you will. Oh, you will. . . .

[15] *See http://en.wikipedia.org/wiki/Mission:_Impossible.*

[16] Our friend Dean Rodney Fong (*http://www.ggu.edu/school_of_law/law_
faculty/full_time_faculty_a_l*) has suggested that you might try matching elements
and facts, using different colors for each matched set. This way, you'd know
when you have established all of the elements for a cause of action. So, for
example, you could underline "breaking" and "broke a window" in red; "entered"
and "entered" in pink; etc.

with the phrase "at night," it also states that Dan wandered around for several hours. Depending on the time of year (and, for that matter, the latitude of where Dan and Vic are located), night could be a very short time (think Alaska in July) or a very long time (Alaska in February). I just can't conclude that the prosecutor can establish the element of "night" as easily as the first two elements, but for the sake of this answer, let's assume that the prosecutor can establish that element. There's still the problem of Dan's "intent to commit a felony therein," and the timing of exactly when he needed the intent to commit the felony.

Dan's lawyer will argue that Dan only broke into the house to get out of the rain. After all, the light drizzle suddenly turned into a downpour, and perhaps there was a real reason that Dan needed to get into a house, rather than just seeking shelter under some sort of overhang. (I can't think of a good reason, though. Maybe he has an irrational fear of rain.) Moreover, Dan didn't try to steal anything from the house, and perhaps he only fired at Vic in self-defense or from some sort of startled reflex. He didn't hit Vic, after all, and Vic had barged in just as Dan was leaving, so perhaps Dan really did just have a surprised reflex. He might not even have realized that he was shooting at *Vic,* given that he shot at the first person coming through the door. Had he known that the person at whom he was shooting was Vic, he would likely have shot several times to follow through with his desire to do Vic ill. The hypothetical says that Dan didn't know that he'd broken into Vic's house, so the prosecutor can't draw the inference that Dan was lying in wait for Vic. How can the prosecutor prove, beyond a reasonable doubt, that Dan was intending to commit a *felony in the house* when he had no idea who lived there? The prosecutor would have to show that Dan intended to commit one of the nine classic felonies: murder, rape, mayhem, robbery, sodomy (in some states), larceny, arson, manslaughter, or burglary (which would be redundant). Dan's lawyer would argue that there aren't enough facts to demonstrate intent for any of those crimes, and that the facts that do exist (as in "shot once and then fled the scene") imply that he didn't know that he was shooting at Vic and that he wasn't trying to kill Vic in the house.

The prosecutor, on the other hand, can argue that Dan's behavior is awfully suspicious, even if Dan didn't know that he was breaking into Vic's house. *Who breaks into a house to get out of the rain?* No reasonable person does that! And Dan had a motive for going after Vic when he saw Vic: "I'll get [Vic] for cheating me out of $100!" (Dan's lawyer, of course, will argue that "get that guy" might well just mean that Dan intended to pursue his legal remedies and sue Vic.) And then there's the matter of the loaded gun that Dan had with him that night. (Dan's lawyer will pipe up, though, that wandering through all sorts of neighborhoods without a loaded gun is stupid—and that carrying one doesn't mean that someone's intending to commit a crime.) Dan did fire a shot in Vic's house, even if he didn't hit Vic. Maybe Dan's just a rotten shot. Certainly, the prosecutor can ask the jury to make a reasonable inference about the following facts: Dan sees Vic, Dan immediately shoots his gun, and after Dan misses, he runs out the door. It's up to the jury to decide if the prosecutor has proven all of the elements beyond a reasonable doubt. I think that there's a decent chance for the burglary charge to go either way.

Note a couple of things about this answer. We didn't fight the hypothetical and argue that there's no way that Dan didn't know that he was in Vic's house. The hypothetical said that Dan didn't know, so we accepted that. (We did, however, show how the prosecutor could get around that little fact without too much trouble.) And we didn't get too bent out of shape that we couldn't come to a conclusion about whether the burglary charge would stick. Once you discuss all of the elements and milk all of the facts for everything that you can, you're done, especially when all that's left is deciding whether a jury would find that a prosecutor has established the elements beyond a reasonable doubt.

4.   Other Exam Issues

There are many other ways to trip yourself up during an exam besides not being mentally or physically prepared for it. You can blow the time allocation; you can focus on "red herrings"; you can misread the questions; and you can have an unexpected crisis. Here are our suggestions for dealing with each of these possibilities.

4.1.   Time Allocation

One mistake that many law students make is actually writing their exam answers too early during the exam. Exam questions are complex and require a significant amount of thinking and preparation time. Nancy almost always followed the same process during every year of law school: She spent one-third of the allotted time for each question reading and rereading the question (and jotting down notes about issues), one-third of the time organizing her answer, and one-third of her time writing her answer in her bluebook.[17] (She's pretty sure that one of her professors gave her this suggestion, and it worked well for her.) Jeff used this same time allotment, based on advice that he received from one of his law professors.[18] Actually, what Nancy would do is read the exam through once, to figure out in which order she'd answer the questions (highest point value questions, also known as highest time allocation questions, first); then she'd go get a drink of water; then she'd go back and read the first question that she was going to answer. Jeff wasn't nearly as obsessive.

To indicate how much of a geek Nancy was, she brought a stopwatch with her to every exam so that she didn't go over her time allocation.[19] Jeff didn't need a separate stopwatch; his regular watch included that function. The beauty of adhering to a strict time allocation process was that, almost always, there was time to proofread the answers and catch mistakes. Don't look ahead, but this *exact same* approach is our recommended approach for answering essay questions on the bar exam.

4.2. Red Herrings in the Hypotheticals

In many law school exams, as in real-life legal problems, there are often irrelevant or distracting facts, which lawyers call "red

---

[17] Don't confuse the bluebooks in which you write exam answers with *the* Bluebook, also known as *A Uniform System of Citation* (*http://www.legalbluebook. com*). Not that you *would* confuse the two, of course.

[18] Nancy was relieved to hear that law professors at several different law schools have given the same advice. Some of her colleagues at one of her former law schools made fun of her for giving this advice to her students. She thought they were wrong then for laughing at the advice, and she still thinks that they're wrong. As a matter of fact, she took her own advice when sitting for the Nevada Bar in 2007, and that advice served her well.

[19] She is only marginally embarrassed by this admission.

herrings." (If you become a securities lawyer, a red herring is that red paragraph on the side of an offering publication. This parenthetical itself, for your purposes, is a red herring. See how it works? It's a distraction.[20])

If we go, once more, to Professor Bateman's burglary hypothetical, we can see what it would look like with some red herrings thrown in:

> *Burglary: "the breaking and entering of a dwelling of another in the nighttime with intent to commit a felony therein."*
>
> One night, when it was raining lightly, Dan went looking for Vic, saying "I'll get that guy for cheating me out of $100." Dan took a loaded pistol with him. **He was wearing blue jeans and a brown T-shirt.** Not knowing where Vic lived, Dan wandered around the city for several hours. Suddenly, it began to rain heavily. Dan smashed a window in the very first house he saw, and entered, **frightening a cat that was napping by the fireplace.** He remained inside the house until the rain stopped. As Dan was about to leave, Vic came in the front door. Startled, Dan pulled out his gun and fired one shot, missing Vic **and hitting a poster of dogs playing poker.** Dan then ran out the door. As it turned out, Dan had broken into Vic's house; Dan did not know whose house it was when he broke in. Dan has been charged with burglary.
>
> What result?

How can you tell that these are red herrings? Well, for one thing, we've **put them in boldface type.** More important, they add nothing to your analysis of the issues in question. It doesn't matter to a burglary charge that Dan shot a poster of dogs playing poker or if he hit the Mona Lisa.

Therefore, when you're preparing to answer this question, your highlighted hypothetical should eliminate those red herrings and look like the original version we produced above. Some professors put red herrings in their exam questions, and others don't. It's perfectly okay for you to ask your professors whether they tend to put red herrings in their exams. Of course, it's also perfectly okay for them to refuse to tell you.

---

[20] Much like many of our footnotes.

4.3. Misreading a Question

Sometimes, even when you spend time reading the question, you'll miss something big. Hey, it happens to everyone. That's one of the reasons we recommend sticking to a strict time allocation. One blown question isn't nearly as bad as one blown question combined with several unanswered questions. If you stick to a strict time allocation, you can try what Nancy did when she realized, with five minutes to go, that she'd misread a question. She kept inserting the word "not" into her answer. She doesn't remember if it helped, but at least it made her feel better.

4.4. Failing to "Read" What Kind of Answer Your Professors Prefer

Different professors prefer different types of answers. Some professors want you to spill out every possible interpretation of every possible fact into as many bluebooks as possible.[21] Others want you to be terse and to the point. Some professors even go so far as to put page limits on each answer.

"Ah," you're thinking to yourself, "but how will I know what type of answer my professor prefers?" Our advice: Go ahead and ask your professors in class if they have a preference. Most professors are willing to give you a direct answer if asked.

All professors, if asked, will admit that they prefer organized answers to rambling, disorganized ones. If you follow our advice, you should have time to write organized answers. If you feel like putting in italicized or boldfaced subheadings to look even more organized, great; you won't be penalized if you don't have hyperorganized answers, but—as with every other part of life—looks can't hurt.

---

[21] Nancy has never understood why her colleagues who prefer these types of answers therefore must prefer to grade exams for days (or weeks) on end, but to each his own.

4.5. Freaking Out or an Unexpected Crisis

There are a million different ways to freak out during exams. You could oversleep the morning of an exam. You could get sick right before an exam; your roommate, loved one, or best friend could get sick right when you need to head off to school. You could have a panic attack in the hallway before the exam. Someone might need to be bailed out of jail, and yours is the only phone number that she's memorized. You can have an adverse reaction to a medication—and maybe not even realize that you're having an adverse reaction because you're hallucinating. (Hey, we bet that you didn't think of some of these. Now you can have even more nightmares. You can thank us later.)

As we recommend in Chapter 8, your law school has built-in mechanisms for dealing with any disaster. When you're in trouble at any time during your law school experience, go see either the Associate Dean for Academic Affairs or the Associate Dean for Student Affairs. Don't go it alone.

5.   Taking Closed-Book and Multiple-Choice Exams

The good news about closed-book exams is that they're typically not as difficult as open-book exams because the professor knows that you don't have easy reference books or notes available. If you followed our advice about memorizing the rules and exceptions to the rules during the semester, then the hardest part of taking a closed-book exam will be no different from the hardest part of taking an open-book exam: applying the facts in the question to the law. If you didn't memorize early, you need to (and we *hate* giving you this advice) cram all of that information so that you can recall it once you start the exam. By not memorizing early, you've just increased your stress level astronomically. Ugh. Get into the exam, open up the exam questions, breathe, and carry on.

Here's what we learned when we were preparing to take the multiple-choice part of various bar exams (the Multistate Bar Examination, or MBE). (We'll talk about the bar exam in Chapter 14.) Because the National Conference of Bar Examiners knows what it's doing,[22] the answers on the MBE will be almost evenly divided among choices A, B, C, and D. Therefore, when we were totally clueless about an answer, we resolved to pick the same letter each time, on the theory that our odds were minutely improved by sticking to a single "we have no clue" answer. Maybe that theory is correct; maybe it's not. But what the theory did for us was encourage us to just pick an answer and move on, so that we could invest our time in answering the questions that we actually had a chance of getting right.

Multiple-choice exams are designed for coverage, and they're time-pressured tests. For you to be successful on a multiple-choice exam, you need to pay attention to the exact words of the question. We suggest that you actually start at the bottom of the question to figure out what the professor is asking. (What the professor is asking is called the "call" of the question.) Then, after you read the call of the question, read the possible answers, and then read the fact pattern of the question. That way, you're more likely to know what to look for in the fact pattern.

Jeff recommends that you approach a multiple-choice exam the same way that you'd read a statute.[23] Obviously, if you know the answer as soon as you read the question, you're simply going to find the correct response, mark it, and move on. If you're puzzled and can't figure out the question, then try to figure out how the various multiple-choice answers differ from each other. Are there specific words that you can find in one of the choices that don't show up in the other choices? Specific phrases? Jeff suggests that, often, you can figure out the "trick" of the question by parsing the wording in each of the answer choices.

---

[22] Contrary to the National Conference of Bar Examiners' expertise, very few, if any, law professors are going to go through the time and trouble to verify that their multiple-choice tests are statistically valid and that the answers are evenly distributed among the possible responses.

[23] In other words, use the plain meaning for words that are not otherwise defined or that do not have a specific industry meaning. If those words are defined so that they have a specific meaning in an industry, use that definition or industry standard.

6.   Writing Answers to Short-Answer Questions or Page-Limited Exams

Nancy gives 72-hour take-home exams (with page limits) in each of her courses, and the trick to doing well on her exams involves prioritizing your answers to make sure that the most important information fits within the space limits. Short-answer or page-limited exams are not the time for you to write novels. Be short and sweet in your answers. Don't use any fluff at all. If your exam answer contains any discussion that's not pertinent to the question, eliminate it.

7.   Some Other Great Resources on How to Take Exams

We're really not trying to kiss up to Aspen Publishers or WoltersKluwer here, but we genuinely like two other books on this subject:

- Charles R. Calleros, *Law School Exams: Preparing and Writing to Win* (2007).
- John C. Dernbach, *Writing Essay Exams to Succeed (Not Just to Survive)* (2d ed., 2007).

Carolina Academic Press also has a good book on the subject: Richard Michael Fischl & Jeremy Paul, *Getting to Maybe: How to Excel on Law School Exams* (1999).

There's also a very funny article written by one of Nancy's former colleagues about truly awful exam-writing techniques. Take a break while you're studying to read C. Steven Bradford, *The Gettysburg Address as Written by Law Students Taking an Exam*, 86 Nw. U. L. Rev. 1094 (1992). You'll feel better. We promise.

CHAPTER EIGHT

The Marathon Aspect of Exams

The truth of the matter is that you always know the right thing to do. The hard part is doing it.

—Gen. Norman Schwarzkopf

Although we're fairly certain that we're starting to sound like a broken record,[1] we're going to repeat ourselves here anyway. Your brain does not perform very well, much less at its optimum potential, if it's trying to function simultaneously with little sleep and too much caffeine. Notwithstanding this well-known fact, many law students walk into their exams thoroughly exhausted and buzzed on caffeine. We believe that these students actively hurt their grades by using such an approach.

For most classes, professors won't give a midterm exam. Therefore, your final examination is your only opportunity all semester—except for class participation credit—to show the professor what you know. You've spent all semester reading and studying in anticipation of this one test. Your grade depends on doing well on the exam. Feel the pressure yet? If not, then you have ice water in your veins, are completely and fully prepared for what is facing you, or haven't figured out what is at stake yet.

Exams are the big time in law school. Most schools have a weeklong "study" time (sometimes called "Dead Week")[2] before launching into a two- or sometimes three-week period of nothing but exams. The stress is so thick in the halls and student lounge that

---

[1] For those of you who have no idea what a broken record sounds like, it kept repeating the same part of a song over and over again because the needle kept sticking to the "groove" in the record. Broken CDs just don't have the same sound. Think of a broken record like the sound that a DJ makes when she samples the same phrase over and over. At least, that's what we think that DJs sometimes do—we don't go to clubs.

[2] We're pretty sure that Dead Week got its name from how you feel at the end of it.

you can cut it with a chainsaw. Most schools will not require you to take more than two exams on a single day, but that still means you may have to take two exams in a single day. Here is a short, sweet plan for dealing with your first semester of exams—and every successive semester's worth of exams.

1.   Sleep: It's Good for You, so Do It Once in a While

All-nighter studying sessions are the subject of myth and legend. But you should avoid them the night before an exam. In this context, learning the volume of information needed to pass an exam is more of a marathon experience than a sprint. (See Chapter 5's discussion of outlining.) Trying to cram a thousand pages of information into your head at the last second is impossible. It's useless. It's counterproductive. Unless you are the next Karl Llewellyn,[3] Elizabeth Warren,[4] Richard Posner,[5] Ahkil Amar,[6] or Dan Bussel,[7] slow and steady will always win the race for you.

Seriously, you need a decent night's sleep before an exam. You want your brain to function at something close to its optimum (stress has a way of impairing your thinking, so you're already at a disadvantage when you walk into an exam). For Jeff, that meant something close to seven hours of sleep. He was used to functioning on considerably less than eight hours, and if he actually managed to stay asleep that long, it seemed to drag him down all day. Everyone is different,[8] so we are not going to try to tell you what you need as far as minimum sleep (we both guarantee that three to four hours is *not* enough). You'll have a good idea of the proper amount for you; just make sure you get pretty close to that amount of sleep the night before an exam.

Remember: Law school exams are not about just knowing the correct answer to the questions. Sometimes, there's not a single

---

[3] *See http://en.wikipedia.org/wiki/Karl_Llewellyn.*

[4] *See http://www.law.harvard.edu/faculty/directory/index.html?id=82.*

[5] *See http://www.law.uchicago.edu/faculty/posner-r/.*

[6] *See http://www.law.yale.edu/faculty/AAmar.htm.*

[7] *See http://www.law.ucla.edu/home/index.asp?page=444* (the smartest person in Nancy's law school class).

[8] Nancy is happiest after nine hours of sleep.

correct answer; sometimes, there are several correct answers. Exams are more about your ability to explain how you got to the correct answer. (Remember proofs in geometry class?[9] Exam answers are as step-by-step as geometry proofs were.) As with geometric proofs, mathematics exams, and some philosophy exams, showing your work here gets you more points toward your grade than simply stating the correct answer. The concept of IRAC[10] will become your new best friend in a law school exam.

Jeff's first-semester Torts exam is a perfect example of the need to be physically ready and mentally organized before you take your exams. First, he had little sleep the night before (maybe two or three hours). He had been doubling up on studying and had another exam in addition to Torts the next day, so he was studying for two subjects the night before the Torts exam. Second, his handwriting was not the most legible (sadly, this is still the case for Jeff—and these were the bad old days when there were no computers for taking tests, just the options of writing or typing). Third, although he had all of the needed answer components as far as elements, facts, and application in his exam answer bluebook, they were not very well explained and were, admittedly, poorly organized. (In fact, his professor wrote the words "verbose" and "poorly organized" on the front page of his exam.)

That verbose and poorly organized piece of work earned Jeff a D for the semester. When Jeff went to review his exam with his professor, the professor refused to amend the grade even though he found all of the required elements, facts, and application of law to facts (i.e., "analysis") needed to receive a B or better on the exam. The review session was not Jeff's idea of fun; the professor was incredibly obnoxious. When Jeff talks about this experience— mostly when his law school asks him for donations—he remembers the lessons that he learned. First, simply throwing everything but the kitchen sink at an exam question will do more harm than good. Second, to make it easy for professors to find all of his analysis, his answers had to be extremely well organized and well–written.

---

[9] Need a refresher on proofs? Take a look here: *http://www.sparknotes.com/ math/geometry3/geometricproofs/section1.html.*

[10] IRAC stands for Issue, Rule, Application, Conclusion. See discussion in Chapter 6.

Finally, the best preparation in the world can be destroyed by a few nights of bad sleep and bad eating habits.

2.   Exercise Helps Vent Your Stress and Keep You Calm

Even assuming that you are getting sufficient sleep and eating a reasonable diet,[11] taking your first-semester law school exams is an especially stressful adventure.[12] You need to find a way to *reduce* the stress that you are under. Not only will your brain work more efficiently, but you'll be better company during the weeks immediately leading up to and including exams. Stated slightly more simply, during Dead Week and even during the last week of classes, the entire law school is showing signs of serious PMS. We're not talking about mild fits of snarkiness; we're talking about knock-down, drag-out screaming matches about who gets what study rooms and when. In essence, craziness ensues, especially among the ranks of first-year students.

Our best advice is to work out all semester and to increase your workouts during Dead Week and exams. When classes are over, your schedule has more free time, and you really will be more efficient at studying if you take a break now and then each day and do something physical. If you can't tear yourself away from studying, listen to some audio study aids or take walks with a study partner. Physical exercise will relieve your stress and will make you a better test-taker. If you don't like going to a gym, why not ride a bike or hike somewhere with a nice view? Even merely standing outside and looking at a nice sunset or sunrise will do wonders for you.

If physical exercise is, however, really not your thing, find a way to get some balance in your life when studying for exams. Read something wholly unrelated to law. Zone out on Facebook. Meditate. Find a way to escape the tension and pressure that surrounds you during exams.

---

[11] Okay, Nancy lived on doughnuts, M&Ms, coffee, and pizza during law school, but (1) she was much younger then, and (2) she would probably have done even better in school had she maintained a better diet.

[12] It seems to get better and a bit less stressful as you go along in progressive semesters, as you get more used to the pressure of the exams.

3.   Substance Abuse Problems

Law students often tend to overuse alcohol and, sometimes, other substances (including memory-enhancing drugs) when they're stressed, especially in social situations (remember how stressful orientation and the first few weeks of classes were?) and during finals. Although it's possible that you can overuse alcohol or other substances for a few weeks and feel no adverse affects, it's more likely that you'll find yourself becoming increasingly dependent on those substances as your stress level increases. Your performance will suffer, which is the last thing that you'll want to happen during exams.

If you're in that group of people for whom a particular substance turns addictive, get help. Addictions aren't the sort of things that you can overcome all on your own. Nor should you even try. (Would you try to overcome near-sightedness on your own? Food allergies?) Addictions are a medical condition, and having an addiction won't keep you from being a practicing lawyer. Not getting the necessary help, however, might keep you from that goal.

4.   The Unexpected Crisis

There are crises that you can avoid (lack of sleep, lack of studying) and then there are real crises that happen (serious illness or death in the family, your own serious illness). Nancy once went to an amusement park right before finals and managed to sprain her neck, necessitating her taking painkillers during exams. Our advice: If there is any chance that your crisis will affect your ability to concentrate fully during exams, go to the Associate Dean for Academic Affairs or the Associate Dean for Student Affairs and ask for an extension. Don't try to tough things out on your own. Schools are very good at helping students in crisis. Ask for help.[13]

---

[13] On the other hand, please don't "cry wolf." If you're feeling just garden-variety stressed out, don't call the dean of students in the middle of the night to get some hand-holding. Use good judgment.

5.   Some Pointers About Clinical Depression

Law students seem to be particularly prone to clinical depression. Nancy herself comes from a family that tends to suffer from it, and she suffers from it. She tells all of her students that she would much rather they reach out to her, even to the extent of calling her at home in the middle of the night, than that she read about them in the next day's obituaries. If you have any of the following signs of depression, go immediately to someone you trust—a professor or the dean of students—to get a referral for a good doctor.

- *Feelings of helplessness and hopelessness.* A bleak outlook—nothing will ever get better and there's nothing you can do to improve your situation.
- *Loss of interest in daily activities.* No interest in or ability to enjoy former hobbies, pastimes, social activities, or sex.
- *Appetite or weight changes.* Significant weight loss or weight gain—a change of more than 5 [percent] of body weight in a month.
- *Sleep changes.* Either insomnia, especially waking in the early hours of the morning, or oversleeping (also known as hypersomnia).
- *Psychomotor agitation or retardation.* Either feeling "keyed up" and restless or sluggish and physically slowed down.
- *Loss of energy.* Feeling fatigued and physically drained. Even small tasks are exhausting or take longer.
- *Self-loathing.* Strong feelings of worthlessness or guilt. Harsh criticism of perceived faults and mistakes.
- *Concentration problems.* Trouble focusing, making decisions, or remembering things.[14]

Antidepressants can take several weeks to kick in fully, so getting started with good counseling is imperative. If you're going to start or change antidepressants, please see your dean of students (or the registrar, if your school doesn't have a dean of students) to make sure that that person can help you with any academic ramifications.

If you're worried about how getting treated for depression will affect your ability to become a member of a state bar, realize that Nancy is a member of five bars (California, Ohio, Nebraska, Texas, and Nevada). Some state bar applications will ask if you've been treated for depression; others won't. What state bar examiners care about isn't whether you have the disease. They care about whether

---

[14] From *http://helpguide.org/mental/depression_signs_types_diagnosis_treatment. htm#signs.*

the disease will adversely affect your ability to represent your clients. And every state bar examiner that we've ever spoken to about this would far prefer that someone get treatment for depression and be able to represent her clients well than avoid treatment to hide her condition.

6.   Collegiality: Play Especially Nice With the Other Students During Exams

Collegiality and physical exercise and tension reduction are critical to maintaining an even affect during exams. (Astronauts used to call it "maintaining an even strain."[15]) Everyone is under pressure. Some people are more driven by internal rather than external stressors, but everyone is nervous about the first set of exams. Maintaining a sense of humor and understanding of what everyone is going through will make you much more likable. Remember, your classmates will be your colleagues down the road, and you don't need to burn too many bridges before you graduate from law school. Who knows when you or your client might need your classmate's help down the road?

7.   Exam-Time Etiquette

7.1. *Law School Exams Are Like* Fight Club

The first rule of Fight Club[16] is that nobody talks about Fight Club.[17] Rule #1 about law school exams is that nobody should talk about the exam in public. Ever. Maybe, just maybe, you can talk about the exam in private, among consenting adults. But it is beyond rude to go down the hall asking someone, "Hey, what about the issue of ABCD? What did you say about that?" Talking

---

[15] *See The Right Stuff* (Warner Bros. Pictures 1983). *See also http://www. entertonement.com/clips/cwvqzhdwmz—Maintain-an-Even-StrainThe-Right-Stuff-Wives-.*

[16] *Fight Club* (20th Century Fox 1999). In fact, postexam life is just like *Fight Club* except (spoiler alert!) without the schizoid ending.

[17] *See http://www.imdb.com/title/tt0137523/quotes.*

about exam questions in public is a lot like talking about salaries in public. Someone is going to go away unhappy. If you can follow this rule, your chances of escaping finals without having a confrontation with one of your classmates will increase exponentially.

7.2. Law School Exams Are Not as Important as Relationships

During at least one of your semesters, someone you know will have a crisis. If you've followed our advice about studying during the semester, you will have the luxury of taking time off during Dead Week and dealing with your friend or family member's crisis. But we're about to say something controversial here. Even if you're completely swamped for time, even if that extra hour or so of studying could make the difference between making a good grade and making an awful grade on an exam, take the time off and deal with the other person's crisis anyway.

Sure, grades are very important. Sure, they'll matter in terms of law review, summer jobs, judicial clerkships, graduating with honors, and even your first job after graduation. But five years after you graduate, you won't even remember your grades. You will, however, remember whether you were a nice person during law school or whether you were a jerk who cared only about yourself; so will your friends and family. Crises are crises in part because they occur at inconvenient times. Life is not all about you. Take care of people who matter to you when they need you. You'll be a better person for it.

CHAPTER NINE _____

First-Semester Grades

*Never give in—never, never, never, never, in nothing great or small,
large or petty, never give in except to convictions of honour and good
sense.*

—Sir Winston Churchill

*Never tell people how to do things. Tell them what to do and they will
surprise you with their ingenuity.*

—Gen. George S. Patton, Jr.

1. First-Semester Grades: The Good, the Bad, and the Ugly

1.1. *If Your Grades Are Uniformly Good, Uniformly Mediocre, or Uniformly Bad*

The good news is that your grades actually are able to tell you
something, whether they're good, bad, or mediocre. They're telling
you about your ability to take law school exams—and they're probably telling you about your relative mastery of the material.

At most law schools, grades are curved, meaning that grades
place you into a pecking order relative to your classmates who took
the same exam that you did. Some of them might have done better
than you; some of them might have done worse. What your grade
tells you is how you did, on the day that you took the exam, relative
to everyone else who took that exam. If the exam was particularly
easy, then the grades might all be bunched around the mean (the
average),[1] with a very small standard deviation from the mean.

---

[1] Nancy's dad, who has read every draft of this book, wants to make it clear
to you that he taught her the difference between a mean and an average.
The "average" actually can refer to a variety of statistical measures, the most
common of which involves adding up a group of numbers and then dividing that
result by how many numbers were in the group. (Nancy wants to point out
that adding up those numbers and then dividing them by how many numbers

If the exam was particularly difficult, then the grades might be more spread out (a bigger standard deviation from the mean). Given the forced bell curve distribution in these classes, grades in such a class don't tell you much about the actual mastery of the material (unless you flunked).[2]

If you happen to be at a school at which grades are clustered into pass/fail, or into High Honors/Honors/Pass/Fail, then (1) pay attention to how your school describes what its grading system means or (2) figure out whether HH/H/P/F is just another way of saying A/B/C/F. If it's the latter, then the preceding paragraph applies.

If your grades are uniformly good, then you've likely gotten the hang of law school exams. Congratulations, and keep up the good work! (Don't slack off!)

If your grades are uniformly bad,[3] it's time to visit the academic support dean and figure out what went wrong. Don't wait for an invitation. Academic support deans are trained in diagnosing whether your problem stemmed from poor exam-taking skills, poor study skills, or a misunderstanding of the law. Academic support is a field, just as Contracts is a field. These people are specialists. Go get help. Do it *now*.

What if you feel like giving up? Hey, we don't blame you for feeling absolutely horrible if you get the first bad grades you've likely ever seen. *Of course* you feel awful. But you need to distinguish the grades (which might be bad) from you (you're not a bad person, right?) and your talents. But now's the time to tough it out—and toughen up a little. Bad grades are a sign that you need

---

are in the group *is* the darn arithmetic mean.) In a discussion about an earlier draft of this book, Nancy's dad sent her the link in Wikipedia discussing this difference: *http://en.wikipedia.org/wiki/Mean*. We love Nancy's dad and promised him that we'd make sure he doesn't get tagged with the fact that Nancy blurs the two concepts.

[2] Nancy *does* flunk students who make scores more than 2.5 standard deviations below the mean grade on her exams. She doesn't care if the students are first-semester first-years or last-semester graduating students. If her name is going on their transcripts and they're that far below the mean, they are not going to pass her course.

[3] Another way to give a professor a nervous tic: Tell her that you studied so hard and put in so much effort that you "deserve" an A. If effort equaled grades in every instance, then Nancy wouldn't have to spend weeks every semester grading each exam. She could just ask her students how much effort each of them put into her courses and mark the exams accordingly.

to change some things, but they're not a sign that you have to switch careers. They're a setback. Acknowledge the setback. Then move forward. As the song goes, "Pick yourself up, dust yourself off, and start all over again."[4]

By the way, if you need to petition the school after one or two semesters of bad grades, for goodness' sake, make sure that your petition sets forth useful advocacy. Write clearly and concisely. Don't demand anything from the school; ask *nicely* for what you want. (You don't exactly have leverage on your side if you're petitioning for readmission, for example, or for the reinstatement of a scholarship after a semester of bad grades.) Speak respectfully about the professor(s) involved. Most important, make sure that you identify how the problem necessitating the petition occurred and how you plan to change your behavior so that you can avoid the problem in the future.

What if your grades are mediocre? By mediocre, we don't mean that you received all A− or B+ grades. (In case you haven't done the math by now, only 10 percent of your class will be in the top 10 percent. The rest of you will be what Nancy calls "Friends of the Coif"[5]—those 90 percent who make the top 10 percent possible.[6]) We mean that you're somewhere below the top one-third of your class but above the bottom one-third of your class. You're smack-dab in the middle.

First off, remember that exam-taking is a skill. You can get better at it with practice. Second, you should also make an appointment with the academic support dean to go over your exam, and you should make an appointment with your professors to see where you went wrong. (Professors will *not* change grades unless they made arithmetic errors in counting up your points. Don't even try. Nancy's been teaching since 1991 and has changed very few

---

[4] See http://lyricsplayground.com/alpha/songs/p/pickyourselfup.shtml.

[5] The Order of the Coif is an honor society at some law schools. See http://www.orderofthecoif.org/. Other law schools might have honor societies like the Order of the Barristers. See http://www.utexas.edu/law/academics/advocacy/boa/barristers.html.

[6] Until The Ohio State University College of Law made Nancy an honorary member of the Order of the Coif so that she could vote on students who were eligible for the Ohio State Coif Chapter, she was a member of the unofficial Friends of the Coif at her own law school. Jeff, on the other hand, was in the top of his class at his law school.

grades, based on miscounting some points.) If your school doesn't have an academic support dean, you might consider dropping by the dean of students for an appointment, if there is one. Finally, don't forget that there are other ways that professors can evaluate you—you can take seminars, for which you write papers; you can take clinics, which involve live-client representation; and you can participate in moot court or mock trial activities. If, after you do everything in your power to get better at taking law school exams, you find that you still can't improve your performance relative to your classmates' performance, then start thinking about ways to diversify your transcript. Participate in moot court, do volunteer work, and come up with other ways to measure your abilities besides exam-taking.

1.2. If Your Grades Are All Over the Place

What if some of your grades are good and some of them aren't? You need to look for patterns. Over the years, Nancy has found that the most common complaint that students make about their exams is that they knew the material cold but still made bad grades. Most of the time, she agrees with them that they knew the material cold. The problem isn't that they were wrong about the material; the problem is that they either didn't know how to apply what they knew to the questions in the exam or they didn't present the material in a manner acceptable to the grader of the exam. (See Chapter 7 on how to take exams.) The first thing that she does to help students diagnose what they did wrong is to diagnose whether the problem is one of poor exam-taking skills or something rather more difficult to fix. Here's how to do that.

If you're allowed to get copies of your exams, then try this exercise: Get some highlighters, and, for each of your exams, highlight the issues that you identified in each answer in one color (say, blue). Then highlight the rules that you used in answer in another color (say, pink). Then highlight the facts from the question that you used in your answer in a third color (say, yellow). Your answers should look like an explosion of preppy colors[7] from

---

[7] *See http://en.wikipedia.org/wiki/Official_Preppy_Handbook.*

summers in the Hamptons.[8] If there's a lot of white space left after you highlight the issues, rules, and facts that you used in your answers, you probably can figure out where you went wrong. If you highlighted the heck out of your answers, there's not a lot of white space left over, and you can't figure out what went wrong, then it's time to see your professors and your academic support dean and get more help in diagnosing what patterns of mistakes you tended to make (e.g., problems in studying or in organizing material).

1.3. If You Have One "Outlier" Grade

Let's assume that most of your grades are good—or at least decent. You have one bad grade. It's eating away at you. It's like a sore that gnaws at the very core of your being. It causes you to lie awake at night. Your self-esteem is suffering. Our survival tip is simple.

It's one grade. You will have many more. Put it behind you. Remember that Jeff received a D in his first-semester Torts class. That grade was an outlier, as he also received the highest grade in Real Property that semester. You can, as he did, put the bad grade behind you and go forth with a renewed focus on doing well. You can even graduate near the top of your class with one bad grade.

Remember, exam-taking is a sport. Athletes make mistakes all the time. The secret to being a good athlete (besides having a lot of skill and practicing obsessively) is the ability to put your mistakes behind you so that you can focus on the present. Your mind needs to be in the present, not in the past. The next section explains why.

2.   Some Advice No Matter How Your Grades Turned Out

2.1. Grades Have Very Little to Do With Your Intelligence or Your Future Abilities as a Lawyer

Let's do a pop quiz. How many of you have asked your doctor how he or she did in medical school? We're guessing that the

---

[8] Neither of us is a preppy, but we hear that the Hamptons is where they go in the summer.

answer is none of you. You take a look at the degrees on the wall and where the doctor is practicing, and maybe you ask the doctor how many of the procedures you're about to get that particular doctor has done. That's it. Grades aren't the issue. Experience and the quality of the doctor's work are the only issues.

Remember that every one of you who got into law school is pretty darn smart to begin with, and grades just express relative ability on one test on a particular day and time. No client will ever ask you to take an exam for him. (If he does, just say no. Taking an exam under another person's name is fraud.) You don't lose brain cells by going to law school, so you're the same amount of "smart" as you were before you matriculated; in fact, you're smarter, because you've learned something about law already. Your future abilities as a lawyer will be determined in part by your legal knowledge, but they'll also be determined in part by your ability to work with people, your ability to understand what makes people tick, your ability to strategize, your ability to write and communicate, your ability to network and negotiate, and (we kid you not) your sense of decency and your sense of humor. You're not going to get graded on all of those, although we do want to remind you (gently) how important your legal writing class will be to your future success as a lawyer.

2.2. Grades Have a Lot to Do With Short- and Intermediate-Term Opportunities (Law Review, Summer Jobs)

We'd be lying if we didn't tell you that, yes, good grades will help you with some of the best perks of law school. Many law schools permit a certain percentage of the students in the top X percent of their class (top 5 percent, top 10 percent, etc.) to "grade on" to the primary law review, so law firms often use membership on the law review as a proxy for good grades. Because many law firms use placement in one's class as a proxy for talent as a budding lawyer, where you end up ranked at the end of your first year could well determine which firms are willing to interview you during your second year of law school.[9] (Personally, we think that

---

[9] When Nancy was the dean at the University of Nebraska College of Law and the University of Houston Law Center, she did what she could to get some

measuring someone's talent as a lawyer based solely on her grades in law school is a lot like measuring her ability as a runner based entirely on her shoe size: If her shoes are exceptionally large or small, maybe that will have some predictive ability, but there are probably many more factors that will go into her running prowess that have nothing to do with her shoe size, just as there will be many more factors that will go into her lawyering prowess that have nothing to do with her grades.)

Whatever grades you have so far, you have. Use them as diagnostic tools, then move on. You can't change the past. But you can use the information from the past to change your future.

2.2.1. Taking advantage of good grades

If you have good grades, great. Go to your Career Services Office, learn how to compose a law school resume, and start figuring out if the current economy will be one that favors hiring first-year law students for summer jobs. Your life is a little easier if you have As (or mostly As) after your first semester (as long as you can keep your grades up). Ironically, the biggest law firms start taking applications from first-years on December 1 of their first year, long before any grades are out. Why? We have no earthly idea.

2.2.2. Making the most of other parts of your resume if you don't have the grades

If you don't have great grades, guess what? You should still go to your Career Services Office, learn how to compose a law school resume, and start figuring out if the current economy will be one that favors hiring first-year law students for summer jobs. You'll just have to do a slightly different job search—one that focuses on

---

law firms to reach further into the class to interview students by explaining that there was very little, if any, qualitative difference between someone in the top 15 percent of the class and someone in the top 20 percent of the class. She argued that the firms were missing out on outstanding candidates by such short-sighted percentage cutoffs. (She still wishes that she could have done even more along those lines.)

other areas of your life. If you've gotten involved in student organizations, your Career Services Dean can help you figure out how
to find alumni who were involved in the same organizations when
they were students. You can also apply to lawyers who are alumni
of your undergraduate or graduate schools. You're looking for
common interests—for connections—and your mission (cue that
Mission: Impossible theme again!) is to figure out who might be
hiring who could be the most sympathetic to your background.
Nancy looked for a summer job in her hometown (but was lucky
enough to receive a job offer from someone who had taught her at
Rice and who had a law firm in Houston). Jeff's first summer job
was with a small insurance defense firm that was not really looking
for a summer associate; more on this later.

2.3.   Grades and Law School Etiquette

If you thought we were serious about not talking about exams
after taking them (and we were), we are even more serious about
not talking about grades in public. Ever. It just isn't done. Let us be
clear. *It just isn't done.* There is no good reason to talk about your
grades in public. Someone will walk away from the conversation
unhappy. If it's you, well, then, maybe you'll learn your lesson. If
it's not you, then you've made someone else miserable. Shame on
you. You might have just made your first real-life professional
enemy. Not good.

2.4.   Grades and the Second-Semester Doldrums

You don't even have to talk about your grades with your classmates to "tell" them how you did. Your behavior, in and out of
class, can send them strong signals. We see the change in behavior
every time first-semester grades come out. Students who never
spoke in class during their first semester will suddenly pipe up
in every second-semester class session; others, whose hands were
permanently raised during the first semester, will slouch in their
seats and never make eye contact with the professor in the second
semester. It's not hard to figure out what grades these two groups
of students received. Believe it or not, most professors don't

remember what grades they gave most of their students,[10] so the behavior shifts are unnecessary and self-defeating.

Then there are the downright snarky students: those who think that their grades, however good, entitle them to be nasty to their classmates. Gosh—we can think of reasons to be nasty to people, but those reasons have nothing to do with law school grades. Instead, those reasons have a lot to do with people who treat others poorly out of an ill-conceived sense of superiority. Hmm. Maybe the snarky students are just students who secretly wish to be treated poorly by their peers. . . . (No, don't give in! Treat them with civility anyway. Take the moral high ground.)

Remember, grades aren't actually the point of law school. Learning about the law—and maybe even learning how to begin to be a lawyer—is the point of law school. So put that transcript out of your mind, whether your first-semester grades made you happy or not. Get back to your primary job: learning about the law.

Need some more encouragement? Then think about this: Last semester, it took you a lot longer to read your assignments than it does now. You're actually more efficient at figuring out what (most) cases say, and you know your way around (some) statutes. You're far ahead of where you were after the first week, or even the first month, of last semester. You've come a long way. That alone is cause for some celebration. And none of that has anything to do with the grades that you got.

2.5. Get to Know Your Professors, No Matter How Your Grades Turned Out

One last nongrade point: Get to know your professors. Sometime in the future, you'll need letters of recommendation from your professors. You might even need those letters 20 or 30 years later. Whether you earned a good grade or a bad grade in the professor's class, the better you get to know the professor outside class, the

---

[10] Professors certainly don't remember the grades they gave most of their students after a few years have gone by. They have enough trouble remembering to which graduating class—or in which graduating *decade*—their previous students belong.

more likely it is that he or she will be able to write a useful letter for you. Nancy has been able to write (honest) letters for some of her students who made horrible grades in her class, saying, "Although [Student X] did not perform well on my exam, I know that she knew the material well, based on our many discussions outside class. Further, I know her to be extremely dedicated. . . ." Jeff's legal writing professor personally introduced him to her former employer, a well-known insurance defense attorney.[11] Jeff then worked for that attorney's firm during the summer between his first and second years and during his second year of law school— all thanks to Jeff's legal writing professor's kind introduction.

---

[11] That attorney became a federal district judge in Ohio a few years later.

CHAPTER TEN

The Upperclass Curriculum

A good plan executed today is better than a perfect plan executed at some indefinite point in the future.

—**Gen. George S. Patton, Jr.**

1. Considerations as You're Choosing Your Upper-Level Courses

Congratulations—you're no longer a first-year law student! That's the good news. Now the *other* good news: Those "required" courses, some of which you probably resented, are mostly behind you, leaving you the freedom to choose the rest of your law school curriculum. (If you're in the evening program at your law school, your upperclass curriculum might be more structured than if you're in the day program, though.)

Which courses should you take? You can get advice from several different people, including your favorite professors, your dean of students and your academic support dean (if your school has one), and any trusted upperclass students. Our advice depends on a variety of considerations. Jeff's school recommended that people strongly consider taking courses that would appear on the Ohio Bar Examination, as the vast majority of his school's graduates practice law in Ohio.[1]

1.1. Your First-Year Class Standing

If you're in the bottom quarter of your class, we strongly recommend that you take courses that correspond to subjects that will be tested on the bar exam that you plan to take. If, however, you did reasonably well in your first year of law school, you can skip this

---

[1] Jeff's law school routinely had one of the highest, if not *the* highest, first-time taker pass rates on the Ohio Bar Exam. Coincidence? Probably not.

section. In Nancy's experience, there is a strong correlation between first-year grades and performance on the bar exam. The correlation isn't perfect (some people at the top of their class fail the bar, and some at the bottom of their class pass), but it's strong enough that you don't want to take chances.

A bar review class is primarily designed to *review* what you learned in law school. If you're a quick study, you can teach yourself some subjects that you didn't cover in law school. (For example, Nancy didn't take wills and trusts or remedies in law school, but she was tested on those subjects on both of the bar exams that she took.[2] Jeff was in the same position, as he didn't take remedies, community property, or family law, and they all showed up on his Texas and Nevada bar exams.) If you didn't get great grades during the first year of law school, don't beat yourself up; on the other hand, do yourself a favor and choose more of the "bar subject" courses in law school. That way, when you *review* them during the bar review course, you don't have the shock of trying to learn all of that material for the first time.

By the way, we've assumed in the previous paragraph that you will be taking a bar review course before you sit for the bar exam. Let's make that assumption explicit. We strongly recommend that you take a bar review course. Which course you take, of course, is up to you. You might want to sign up to be a bar review course representative during your first year of law school to get the course for free for yourself. Or you might just wait to see which course makes sense to you as you approach your bar exam preparation. Learning the material necessary to pass the bar is far too onerous to do on your own. Don't tough it out. If it's at all economically feasible for you, take a course, and take that course seriously. For more on the bar exam process, see Chapter 14.

1.2.   Your Interests

If certain types of courses intrigue you, take them. Most law students don't have a clue about what type of lawyer they want to be after graduating, and the best way to figure out what interests

---

[2] At least she has a vague memory of having been tested on those subjects. Repression is a useful psychological tool.

you is to experiment by taking a lot of different subjects and seeing what captures your attention.[3]

1.3. Your Favorite Professors

If you enjoyed taking a particular professor's class as a first-year law student, take more of that professor's courses as an upper-class law student, no matter what that professor teaches. At least you know that you'll enjoy the professor's teaching style. Some of your professors might even turn out to be friends or good business contacts down the road.

1.4. Subjects That Are Too Ugly to Learn on Your Own

Certain subjects are very complicated. Could you study them on your own and master them? Probably. But why would you want to do that, when you could take a course that will give you a conceptual framework to help you understand the subject? Our nonexhaustive list of these "too ugly to learn on your own" subjects includes the following:

- Federal Income Tax
- Corporate Tax
- Administrative Law
- ERISA[4]
- Conflict of Laws

1.5. Your Law School's Strengths

If your school has a particularly strong curriculum in an area (or in a couple of areas), take advantage of that strength. Aside

---

[3] Don't be surprised, however, if you find out, when you're a practicing lawyer, that you guessed wrong. Nancy was convinced that she wanted to be a securities lawyer until she became one. She was also convinced that she would hate being a bankruptcy lawyer. She was wrong on both counts.

[4] ERISA stands for the Employee Retirement Income Security Act of 1974 and its amendments.

from reading your school's promotional materials and the *U.S. News & World Report*'s specialty rankings, both of which will have their flaws, look to see how many faculty members[5] teach in a subject area, along with any specialty law journals in that area and how many courses are (regularly) offered in that area. Especially in a tight job market, having a specialty gives you an edge at graduation.

1.6. Prerequisites

Every course isn't offered every semester, and some courses are prerequisites for other courses. Pay attention to prerequisites, as missing one puts you out of sequence, which is difficult to fix.

1.7. A Short List of Courses That Jeff and Nancy Believe to Be Exceptionally Useful

Although we're sure that we're going to leave some great courses off this list, here are some courses that we think that every well-educated law student should take:[6]

- Evidence
- Federal Income Tax
- Business Organizations
- Family Law
- Criminal Procedure
- Administrative Law
- Secured Transactions

---

[5] Don't forget to include adjunct professors as well as tenured and tenure-track professors in your count.

[6] This list is exclusive of the first-year curriculum that might include Contracts/Article 2 (Sales), Real Property, Civil Procedure, Criminal Law, and Constitutional Law, as well as the upper-level (and typically required) Professional Responsibility course.

To this list, Jeff would add Negotiable Instruments and Bankruptcy.[7] Nancy would, instead, add Environmental Law and Employment Law.

1.8. Classes You Might Want to Consider if You're Planning to Clerk After Law School

- Federal Courts (if you're thinking about applying for a federal clerkship)
- Any advanced Constitutional Law courses
- Criminal Procedure
- Evidence
- Conflicts of Law
- Administrative Law

2.   Joint-Degree Programs

On the theory of "in for a dime, in for a dollar," you might want to consider getting a joint degree (adding a second degree to your JD) while you're in law school. The most common joint degree is the JD/MBA, but there are all sorts of other joint degrees, such as the JD/MSW (master's in social work), the JD/PhD, and even the JD/MD, although not every joint degree is offered at every school.

Why get a joint degree? We're all for additional education and credentials, and depending on what you want to do with your degree, you might want to have, say, more of a business background or more of a social work background. In addition, a joint degree will shave some time off both degrees: For example, the three-year JD and the two-year MBA combine to take only four years as a JD/MBA.

Reasons not to go for the joint degree, besides the extra time and expense, include not graduating with your entering class and

---

[7] Jeff's list is suspiciously similar to the vast majority of topics that appear on most state bar examinations.

spending one entire year away from your law school classmates. (Typically, you spend one year in law school, the next year in your other degree program, and the rest of your time taking courses in both programs.) If you don't have a particular drive to get a second degree concurrent with your JD program, then don't; but both of us wish that we'd gone for joint degrees. It's much more difficult to go back to school later to get the additional degree.

3.   Cocurricular Activities

Now that you're an upperclass student, you might decide to pursue some cocurricular activities, such as law review/law journal or moot court. We each did law review; Jeff did moot court and mock trial. There are a lot of good reasons to add cocurricular activities to your law school experience. You gain expertise, you interact with people whom you otherwise might not have met, and you add some useful entries to your resume.

Make no mistake, though. Each of these activities involves hard work. Nancy spent her entire third year working on law review, often to the exclusion of everything else. Jeff's moot court practices took several hours a day. If you're not going to commit the time to do the activity well, don't do it at all, because your colleagues will resent you for shirking. Years later, each of us can still list everyone who dropped the ball in law review, because every dropped ball meant more work for us.

Some law reviews are "grade-on" memberships, meaning that only the top X percent of a class will qualify. Others are "write-on," meaning that students who wish to join will have to perform certain tasks that are graded by the law review's current members. Still others use a combination of the two methods to choose their members. Our advice for the write-on competitions? If Bluebooking[8] is involved at all, pay attention to the Bluebook rules. Bluebooking is some of the most annoying scut work that a law review member has to do, but it's a skill that every law review member must master. And because most write-on competitions

---

[8] See http://www.legalbluebook.com.

involve writing a paper, or a first draft of a paper, make sure that yours reads well, demonstrates solid analysis and research, and is meticulously proofread. Law review is, in the end, a magazine, and the people who staff it need to be good writers.

If you join any organization during law school, at some point, you'll need to consider whether you want to take on a leadership role in that organization. Leadership roles include editorial boards of law reviews and officer positions (president, vice president, etc.) in other organizations. Again, the experience in leading an organization can be extremely useful for you, because lawyers have to have good people skills; on the other hand, leadership roles are very time-consuming. There are trade-offs in law school, as in life, so if you're planning on taking on a leadership role, something else in your schedule has got to give a little (or a lot).

4. Etiquette in Your Upper-Level Courses

You'll be tempted to slack off a bit in your second and third years (and fourth year, if you're an evening student). After all, you're a lot busier now than you were as a first-year student. ABA rules permit you to work up to 20 hours per week while attending school full-time (or to work full-time if attending school part-time), and you might also be working on a law review, doing moot court, running a student organization, job hunting, or dealing with other time constraints, such as family obligations. In fact, you're likely dealing with more than one of these additional tasks.

Luckily, your studying is far more efficient now. You can read cases and statutes much more quickly and you're likely getting more out of your reading. (You *are* still reading the assignments, right?) But with all of your other responsibilities, you might find yourself tempted to skip classes or to do your other work during class.

As we discussed in more detail in Chapter 3, be aware that if you can see your professor, that professor can see you just as well—and can tell if you're paying attention in class. If you wouldn't go to a work meeting and check e-mail while your boss was talking with you, don't do that during class, either. (If you *would* check e-mail in front of your boss, then we're going to go out on a limb here and guess that you don't have the best of relationships with your boss or that your family owns the business.) If you wouldn't sit in a work meeting with your arms crossed in front of your chest wearing a grumpy look on your face, then don't sit that way in class. If you resent going to class, then don't go. (But you might want to do a little calculation that we like to call the tuition-dollar-per-class-hour calculation. If you skip class, at least be aware of what that's costing you—or whoever's paying your tuition.) Also remember that some upper-level classes also include a participation component. It's hard to get participation points if you're not actually *in* the classroom.

5.   Options for GPA Enhancement in the Upperclass Curriculum

Let's say that your first-year GPA isn't what you'd hoped it would be. As an upperclass law student, you now have the opportunity to choose some of your courses based on how the professor will evaluate your performance. Not all law school courses use exams to evaluate you. Some courses require you to write papers, or conduct a trial, or represent mock (or live) clients. You might have strengths that you haven't discovered yet, and non-exam ways of evaluating you might just showcase those strengths and improve your GPA in the process.

6.   Scheduling Your Life

A typical upperclass, law review, moot court, and work schedule for Jeff looked a lot like his first-year schedule, except he had more free time on weekends (see chart in Appendix C). He was much more efficient in his studies and class preparation, reducing his preparation time from 1.75 to 2 hours per class meeting to approximately 1 hour per class meeting, but his total time committed to law-school-related work (including extracurricular activities) was only slightly less hectic than what he was doing his first year.

Nancy, not surprisingly, wasn't as structured in her schedule. She worked out almost every day, she typically worked on law review most afternoons and evenings, and she read for classes in the mornings. She also napped a lot, became a power-lifter, worked as a "techie" in several plays, and generally escaped the law school part of the campus several times a week. The upperclass curriculum wasn't nearly as stressful for her as her first-year curriculum was, although she missed the camaraderie that came from the "fear factor" of the first year. Isn't it amazing what a single year of experience can do for your perspective?

7. A Few Words About Your Final Year of Law School

If you think about your second year (or second and third years, for evening students) as the time for building your foundation for understanding the law, then you can use your final year for creating the transition to the practice of law. Let's say that you take the traditional foundation courses—Evidence, Federal Income Tax, and Business Organizations—during your second year. Your last year could provide you with more depth in these areas. For example, if you enjoyed Evidence, you could take Pretrial Advocacy or Trial Advocacy in your last year. If you discovered that you liked Federal Income Tax or Business Organizations, you could take Corporate Tax or Securities Law to build your skill set.

You should also consider using your last year to fill some holes in your education. We strongly recommend that you take an accounting course if you're not familiar with the basics of accounting. We know, we know: You came to law school to avoid the number-crunching of business school. But we know of no lawyers who avoid accounting issues in practice.[9]

So if you're weak in statistics, learn it. If you're fuzzy on microeconomics, learn it. You can typically take up to six hours of graduate-level courses in other departments that can count toward

---

[9] We actually edited two books that highlight what happens when lawyers are hornswoggled by a failure to understand accounting. *See* Nancy B. Rapoport, Jeffrey D. Van Niel, & Bala G. Dharan, *Enron and Other Corporate Fiascos: The Corporate Scandal Reader*, 2d (2009) and Nancy B. Rapoport & Bala G. Dharan, *Enron: Corporate Fiascos and Their Implications* (2004).

your JD degree. Don't wait until you're out in the real world to catch up on areas that will help your law practice.

Finally, start shifting your mindset during your last year. Maybe you've decided that your papers need only be "good enough" in law school, because law school isn't "real life." But "good enough" work in real life is not acceptable at the highest levels of law practice. (Would you want your doctor to do a "good enough" job examining you?) Get into the habit of asking yourself what your clients and colleagues would want from you, and then perform to that level. Trust us: You'll stand out if you take your work seriously, even before "real life" begins.

While you're in that transition from law school to the real world, you should consider what kind of lawyer you want to be. We don't mean that you should focus on a legal specialty. We mean that you should spend some time thinking about whether you're going to be the type of lawyer who works in his or her community, who volunteers to do pro bono work, and who sets a good example to repudiate the public's low opinion of lawyers. Both of us have done volunteer work, and both of us have done pro bono work, and we have really enjoyed using our legal skills to help others for free. Get geared up now to ask yourself if you're willing to set aside some of your precious (and it *is* precious) free time to help others.

CHAPTER ELEVEN.

Summer Jobs

I have just taken on a great responsibility. I will do my utmost to meet it.
—Adm. Chester W. Nimitz

1.   Searching for a Summer Job

The desire to get the right summer job can be so time-consuming that it can literally become an all-encompassing quest—one that defeats your day-to-day job of learning the law. We know that finding a summer job is important. You need experience, and you need an income. Do everything in your power to find gainful employment, but don't forget your most important job: learning the law. That said, there are two ways to find summer jobs: on-campus interviewing (for a very few students), and every other way (for the rest of you).

Your career services office will know all of the timelines that you and any potential employers should follow (the "NALP guidelines").[1] What might surprise you is how quickly the job search process can begin. Depending on when grades come out at your law school, you might be searching for jobs even before all of your first-year grades are available, and while you're still choosing your second-year courses.

2.   On-Campus Interviewing, or Statistics 101 Revisited

Most law firms that participate in on-campus interviewing (OCI) are looking for students in the top 10 to 25 percent of their class. At most law schools (at least until the recession), many, if not most, graduates had jobs within nine months of graduation, which meant that at least 75 percent of the students (those not in the top

---

[1] *See http://www.nalp.org/fulltextofnalpprinciplesandstandards.*

10 to 25 percent of their class) had to have gotten their jobs outside the OCI process.

If you are in that small group of students who is able to use OCI, great! But recognize that OCI will work best if you want to work at one of the employers participating in OCI—if you want to go to an area not covered by those employers, such as a different geographic area or a different type of employer, then you're going to have to do the type of legwork that everyone who doesn't participate in OCI has to do.

For those of you who will participate in OCI, your class rank will, in most instances, directly control what interview slots are made available to you.[2] Typically, OCI allows you to submit a resume to certain employers and hope for an interview. You might be able to "bid" for interviews based on an allocation of "points" that you get at the beginning of interview season. (Different career services offices operate differently.) But employers receive many more resumes than they have jobs, and most of these employers are also interviewing at multiple schools. As such, submitting your resume is merely the first step in the chain to getting a job. Getting an interview is the second step.

3.   Stupid Interviewing Mistakes That Students Make

3.1.   Stupid Resume and Social Networking Mistakes

Before you even get through the door, you can make stupid interviewing mistakes. Make sure that your e-mail address is professional-looking. Avoid e-mail addresses like these:

- hunkahunkaburninglove@gmail.com
- bigbabe@yahoo.com
- lovestodrink@hotmail.com

---

[2] The father of one of Jeff's classmates owned an extremely well-known and profitable real estate business in the same city in which the law school was located. Not surprisingly, that classmate had no difficulty getting interviews for firms, regardless of his class rank. Unless you are in a similar position, your class rank will likely determine for which interviews you qualify.

Beware the unflattering Facebook or other social network-ing post or photo. Employers will Google you, and they are completely within their rights to reject you for having the bad taste to show your sophomoric online side, even though you showed that sophomoric side when you were, in fact, just a sophomore. The Internet is *forever*. Be very careful about what you post online, and if your friends post something unflatter-ing about you online, do everything in your power to per-suade them to remove it. If they balk, then they're not your friends.

We should add a word about blogging and commenting on blogs. Nancy loves blogging. She has her own blog (*http://nancyrapoport.blogspot.com/*), and she's a frequent poster and com-menter on other blogs. But she also had an established career before she started blogging, and she's careful to post only those comments that she can back up with facts or mark clearly as her own opinion. On top of that, she's feisty and is comfortable being criticized. If you don't already have an established legal career (if you did, would you be reading this book?), be very careful about blogging and commenting on blogs.

3.2. Making Your Resume Too Short

Although the common wisdom is that your resume should not exceed one page, many people have done enough before law school—prior careers, significant travel, additional degrees—to justify having at least a two-page resume. Use your judgment. If you have had an interesting life so far, use your experiences to your advantage.

Don't forget to put something on your resume that gives an interviewer something with which to start the interview. If you have an unusual hobby, listing that hobby (Nancy's hobby in law school was power-lifting) gives even the shyest of interviewers a conversation starter. If you've had a previous career (Jeff was an Ohio State Trooper before law school), list that career. Listing something unusual will help you stand out from the crowd and should get a good conversation started, too.

3.3. Not Researching the Employers With Whom You're Seeking a Job

Yes, we know that, for most of your law school admissions essays, you wrote something on the order of "I have always wanted to attend [insert name of school]" and then did a mail merge. That trick won't work for employers, who are looking at many students at numerous law schools for their scarce job slots. Take the time to look over the employers' materials, much of which can be found on their Web sites. Not every employer practices every type of law, and interviewees have been known to make boneheaded mistakes by stating that they want to practice in an area that an employer just doesn't "do" (or worse yet, "does" but on the opposite side from the side that the interviewee mentions).[3] Do your homework.

3.4. Personal Grooming Mistakes

Your family and friends might love you for the person you are. Employers don't. So don't take the risk of dressing for your own comfort. Dress conservatively. Wear a suit—and make sure that it fits. (You don't have to spend a lot of money on a nice suit, but it would be a good idea to go to a tailor if you need to have the sleeves or hem altered. Nancy loves shopping for suits at consignment stores.) If you're wearing a skirt suit, then make sure that everything's covered nicely when you're sitting down.[4] As one of Nancy's colleagues has observed, you—not your clothes—should be memorable. You don't want the interviewer remembering you as "that tie guy" or "that red flower gal." As Coco Chanel said, "Dress shabbily, they notice the dress. Dress impeccably, they notice the woman."[5] If you don't feel particularly fresh, even though you

---

[3] For example, don't tell a plaintiffs' firm that you've always wanted to defend large corporations (or vice versa).

[4] Nancy wishes that she'd followed her own advice one day when she was introducing Justice Breyer on TV and then sat down, only to watch her skirt ride up, slowly but steadily, during the Justice's speech. Luckily, the speech ended before Nancy's skirt—and career—did.

[5] http://www.quoteland.com/author.asp?AUTHOR_ID=2338.

showered in the morning, do a quick "pit-wash" in the restroom before your interview. You're going to be in an interview room for around 20 minutes. If there's a smell in the room, you don't want to be its point of origin.

3.5. Having a Bad Handshake

Look your interviewer in the eye when shaking hands, and for goodness' sake, have a proper handshake. No dead fish or bone-crusher handshakes, please. If you don't know if you have a proper handshake, then ask someone in the career services office to evaluate yours.

3.6. Stupid Questions During the Interview

Until you've been offered the job, don't ask questions that presume that you have the job in hand already. In other words, if you don't have a job offer, it's too early to ask about salaries, partnership tracks, bonuses, sabbaticals, and other benefits. Think of the pre-job-offer stage like the first few dates. You wouldn't ask your date about his or her thoughts about babies, would you? Salaries and benefits are the employer version of babies. What you should be asking about is how you'll be getting assignments and how you'll be evaluated. Those types of questions are fair game.

3.7. Not Having Any Questions Prepared for the Interviewer

You should have some questions ready for the interviewer, and at least some of these questions should be specific to the potential employer. Others, however, can be more general. For example, you should be prepared to ask how the employer doles out assignments and how those assignments get evaluated. After all, you care about how you'll be trained and how you'll get feedback. You might consider asking the interviewer how she decided on her career path or what she likes best about the people with whom she works.

3.8.   General Rudeness

Turn off your cell phone before the interview.[6] Unless you have a bona fide family emergency (someone in your family is dying or, alternatively, about to give birth), there is nothing more important during your interview than the interview itself. Give the interviewer your full attention. Don't text anyone during the interview. At the end of the interview, thank the interviewer for taking the time to meet with you (even if the interview itself was miserable). Write a follow-up thank you note. If you go on a callback interview, you'll need to write a thank you note to everyone with whom you met, and it's a nice touch to write a thank you note to the employer's recruitment coordinator as well, if someone coordinated the interview day for you.[7]

By the way, if you happen to be a Gen X/Gen Y/Gen Z person, please be aware that many senior decision makers are more comfortable with formality and hierarchy than you are. They[8] are used to face-to-face conversations (as opposed to e-mails), being treated with deference and respect, and a type of 8-5 work ethic that values "face time" (meaning time in the office). Wait for the partner or senior lawyer to ask you to call him by his first name. Even if you believe that you're entitled to as much respect as the senior partner is, wait until you're in a position of power to demand that respect. Your interview is *not* that time. Neither is your summer job.

Oh, and one more point for dealing with old geezers like us: The correct response when someone says "Thank you" is to say, "You're welcome." Not "no worries." Not "no problem." Saying a simple "you're welcome" will make us feel all warm and fuzzy for having thanked you.

3.9.   Bad-Mouthing Previous Employers

If interviews are like dating, bad-mouthing previous employers is like bad-mouthing previous romantic partners. If you're asked

---

[6] Also, don't flash a nicer cell phone than the one that the recruiter is using.

[7] You'll know if there's a recruitment coordinator. He'll identify himself as such before you arrive and will likely be your first contact during your callback.

[8] And by "they," we're including ourselves.

why you left your previous employment, be truthful—even if you didn't leave on positive terms—but try not to be malicious. No one gets along with everyone in an office or business, so having a personality conflict with someone is not fatal to getting a job. However, bad-mouthing a prior employer is a signal that you'd bad-mouth a future one.

3.10. Trying to Be Too "Cool" at the End of the Interview

If you want the job, say that you want the job. Too many people make the mistake of assuming that, if they're interviewing, the employer will intuit that they want the job. Enthusiasm is always appreciated. In a sense, by saying that you want the job, you're affirming the interviewer's own choice of employer. (After all, you want to work where the interviewer's working.)

3.11. Skipping Too Many Classes for Callbacks

Yes, we want you to get a summer job, and we know that most callbacks are day-long affairs. If you have to fly to another part of the country for a callback, you might have to miss several days of class. But use your judgment. Don't go on so many callbacks that you return to all of your courses completely and utterly lost. Flunking your fall courses won't help you get a summer job. Because you could well miss some classes, make arrangements in advance. Are you going to ask some of your classmates for their notes? Will some of your professors let you audiotape their classes? Plan ahead.

4. Stupid Interviewing Mistakes That Interviewers Make, and How You Might Want to Deal With Them

4.1. Illegal Questions

Even though lawyers should know better, they'll often ask illegal questions: questions about marital status, religion, pregnancy, and the like. You could refuse to answer these questions, and you'd be within your rights, but typically, the interviewer isn't being malicious, just stupid. More likely than not, the interviewer is trying to get to a job-related question but doesn't know how to ask the question without putting his foot in his mouth. If the interviewer is asking about religion, perhaps he's asking whether you're able to travel for business on weekends or whether you'd be able to staff an office located in a country not known for religious tolerance. You could answer that type of question with "I see that you might be interested in whether I'd be able to travel on Fridays. Here's what I'm able to do. . . ." A question about marriage or children might be a question about whether you can handle a brutal work week. Again, you can respond by saying, "I can see that you're wondering whether I'm able to juggle my responsibilities. Here's how I'm able to juggle them while taking 16 credit hours, working 20 hours per week, and. . . ."

When Nancy was interviewing for deanships, she was of childbearing age, and she knew that the law faculties (and the provosts) were wondering whether she and Jeff were going to have a passel of kids during a deanship. She also knew that such questions were illegal and that, therefore, such questions were unlikely to come up during her interviews. So she raised them herself (not illegal), by saying, "I'll bet that you're wondering if we're planning to have children while I'm deaning." She raised the issue for two reasons: one was to talk about the issue generally, and one was to see how the schools would react to her statement.

The main point here is that there will be some issues that are deal-breakers for you. You might care about how LGBT-friendly[9] an employer is; you might indeed have a family member in need of special care; you might have religious restrictions that would affect certain of your work hours. If something is important to you but illegal for your interviewer to ask, nothing prevents *you* from bringing it up yourself. If the ensuing discussion indicates that you wouldn't be a good fit, then you've saved yourself some heartache. On the other hand, the ensuing discussion might surprise you—in a good way.

---

[9] LGBT stands for lesbian, gay, bisexual, and transgendered.

4.2. Bad Interview Skills

Bad interviewer horror stories abound: interviewers who answer their cell phones during the interview; interviewers who never look at the candidate for the entire 20 minutes; interviewers who just stare; interviewers who just talk about themselves and never ask any questions; interviewers who key all of their questions toward stereotypes of the interviewees. The good news is that you'll have great stories to tell after these interviews are over. Moreover, 20 minutes isn't a lifetime, and you can still practice your skills, even on the worst of interviewers. Try to draw the interviewer out. Try to steer the interview toward a useful topic of conversation. If all else fails, stare back. (Hint for staring back: Don't stare at the person's eyes; stare at the person's eyebrows. It looks as if you're staring at the eyes, but it's less unnerving for you.) And remember this joke, if you find someone who has such bad social skills that she never even looks up to greet you: What's the difference between an introvert [insert statutory subject matter here] lawyer and an extrovert [same subject matter] lawyer?[10] The extrovert looks at *your* shoes while talking.

5.   Substitutes for Summer Jobs

5.1. Research Assistantships

Your professors might need help over the summer in doing their research for their articles or books. Nancy always hires research assistants for the summer, and the law school sets the hourly pay rate. If you've enjoyed a professor's course, ask the professor if she hires research assistants, and then submit a resume and writing sample early. Some professors post a job opening with the career services office, and others just go by word of mouth. Be aggressive (but nicely so). If you're interested, say so. Often, by doing a good job as a research assistant, you'll have a good reference for life.

---

[10] Nancy prefers to make fun of ERISA lawyers in this joke. The original joke involves accountants, not lawyers.

5.2. Unpaid Clerkships and Externships

Jeff has been an unpaid extern himself (in both college and law school), and has hired several such externs as an attorney. Unpaid work experience is, in some cases, a superb opportunity to get your foot in the door and get to know a potential employer. If you are fortunate enough to have the opportunity to do substantive work at your clerkship or externship, that experience might help you expand or narrow the types of law that you are willing to consider following your graduation from law school. Check with your career services office and your dean of students about these opportunities. Don't be surprised if your law school only lets you apply to nonprofits and government internships or externships. You probably can't get course credit for working in the private sector. And not all private-sector employers will let you volunteer. There might be a whole host of reasons to say "no" to your offer to volunteer: legal reasons, logistical reasons, and staffing (supervising) reasons. On the other hand, as Nancy's fearless mother has said, "If you don't ask, you can't get." It can't hurt to ask any employer for a volunteering opportunity. No one's died from a "no" response, based on our records.

5.3. Summer School (Including Summers Abroad)

Like to travel? Can't find a summer job? Want to get some law school credits out of the way? You might want to consider taking summer school courses at an ABA-accredited summer school program. You don't necessarily have to take your own school's summer school program, although you'll want to check with your school about how other schools' courses would transfer. Especially if your own school doesn't offer courses in an area in which you're particularly interested, you might want to consider taking those courses elsewhere.

Summer school isn't cheap, especially if you're going to be living in another city. You'll be paying tuition and fees in addition to your living expenses, and your credits will only be recorded as a "pass" (assuming you earn a certain threshold grade). But if you have wanderlust and you can afford it, you might want to try some international programs.

5.4. Nonlaw Jobs

You have to eat. Especially in the summer between your first year and your second year, if you're a day student, getting any sort of job is fine. Don't worry if you can't get a law-related job. You'll have another summer to try for one, and, if you get a judicial clerkship after graduation, you'll have an additional summer after you graduate for yet another summer job.

5.5. Other Pointers

Don't forget to drop off your most recent resume at your career services office before you leave for winter break. You never know what might happen while you're recovering from exams. You should also leave a copy of your most recent resume with non-law-school friends and family. Networking is always a good thing.

6.   Success at Your Summer Job

Success at your summer job requires several overlapping skill sets. These skill sets include social skills, your work ethic, and your writing and researching skills.

6.1. Stupid Summer Job Tricks: Avoid Making These Mistakes at All Costs

As Nancy's dad always says, "You only get one chance to make a first impression." Make yours a good one.

6.1.1. Treating people poorly

Be nice to everyone. The support staff not only knows more than you do (yes, even more than you do about the practice of law) but can make you or break you when it comes to those little things like showing you the ropes. Nancy has worked as a secretary before, and one of her best friends is her former judge's second secretary. Secretaries can make your life easier or more difficult. Don't for a second think that secretaries aren't smart. They are. They often can help you out with proofreading, Bluebooking, and strategizing. If you tell them what you need, they often can come up with a better way of organizing your work than you might be able to do on your own. If you treat them as the professionals that they are, your work might move up in the pile. Treat them as if they're somehow less important than you are, and your work will get done sometime after the next Ice Age. The same thing is true of everyone from the people in the mailroom to the people in the coffee shop down the street.[11] People talk to each other, and you never know who's friends with whom. Now you know why your parents taught you always to be nice—or at least polite—to everyone.

6.1.2.   Getting an assignment wrong, doing it poorly, or turning it in late

If you don't understand your assignment, ask questions.[12] If the person giving you the assignment is not good at explaining what you're supposed to do, find someone else to explain it to you, or at the very least, cover your butt by asking questions in e-mail or in explaining your assumptions as you write your memo (which is what most of your assignments will be, at least at law firms). And make sure to proofread your assignment before you hand it over. Even if someone asks for a draft, don't hand over a first draft. As Nancy's dad used to tell the new hires at his plant at DuPont, "When you were in grad school, you had exams every once in a while; at work, though, every day is an exam, and every day, you're getting evaluated. The first six months can determine the path of your entire career."

If you think that you might be late in getting your assignment finished, don't wait until the last minute. Tell the person for whom the assignment is due that you're having problems finishing the assignment on time, explain why, and see whether it's more

---

[11] Oh, you don't think that the kid at the coffee shop knows the senior partner at your law firm? Who do you think that kid's mom *is*, anyway?

[12] Most firms will assign you a mentor (or even more than one) for the purpose of helping to resolve some of these types of issues. When in doubt, ask for help.

important for you to be a little late and thorough or to be finished on time and not as thorough in your work.

What if you have assignments with competing deadlines? It's not really up to you to decide which assignment is more important. It's up to the people who gave you those assignments. Let them know that there are competing deadlines, and then let them duke it out as to whose assignment gets priority.

6.1.3. Treating social events as, well, social events

Your employer will have social events scheduled from time to time over the summer. RSVP (that's French, by the way, for *répondez, s'il vous plaît*, which means "respond, if you please") on time, and if you say you're going, then go. If the invitation lets you bring a guest, then bring one—but only bring someone whose behavior at social functions you can trust.[13] Your employer is watching your behavior in each of these social settings, so getting drunk is *a very bad idea*, as is wearing provocative clothing, propositioning anyone, or telling anyone "what you really think" about him or her, unless what you really think is rather flattering.[14]

6.1.4. Assuming that the summer program is anything like the regular (nonsummer) world

It's quite possible that, in the real world, people don't go out to two-hour lunches and leave work before 8 p.m. If you want to find out what work is actually like after the summer program has ended, ask the people there with whom you've developed a good relationship. Better yet, come into work early some mornings and stay late some evenings. Come in on some weekends. See who's there and what each of them is doing. Observation is often better than conversation when it comes to discovering what really goes on.

---

[13] Jeff made this mistake at a firm function for one of the firms where he worked as a summer associate. His date for the night (whom he had only dated *once* before that night) picked up the lead singer in the band. Needless to say, that incident is still discussed at that firm when "bad dates" are the topic.

[14] And isn't harassment.

6.1.5. "Blamestorming"

At some point over the summer, you'll make a mistake. Own up to it, fix it as best you can, and that mistake won't be fatal. Blame someone else, however (*see http://www.youtube.com/watch?v=7Z-tHzc7VXU*), and you've made an enemy for life. Never—under any circumstances—blame someone who's on the support staff for a mistake. When you're an attorney, you're responsible for supervising those who report to you, and that means, in part, that you're responsible for supervising their work. Even if someone who reports to you did make a mistake, it's *your* mistake for failing to catch his mistake or fix it in time. Our motto for having a loyal team: Share the success and take the blame.

6.2. *Make Sure That You Get Feedback*

Often, the people who give you assignments are so busy that they forget to evaluate you. One of the most important lessons that you can learn is that you, not they, are responsible for your own career. If someone has reviewed your work and hasn't given you feedback, you should find a time (convenient to the person who gave you the assignment) to get feedback.[15] One way to get feedback is to ask the attorney if he needs any follow-up. If you've tried to get feedback, and you still can't, then you need to let someone else know. On the other hand, if you keep getting assignments from the same person, that's probably a good sign that your work is decent.

Let's put it this way: Summer jobs (like so many other things in law school life) are like dating. If no one's giving you feedback during the time when everyone's supposedly on his best behavior, what are the odds that you're going to get feedback if you work there "for real" after law school?

---

[15] Before law school, we used to use the phrase "constructive feedback," but law school has ruined the word "constructive" for each of us.

7.   After the Summer Job's Over

7.1.   If You've Gotten an Offer

Congratulations! That's great news! But you can't rest on your laurels yet. For one thing, you need to know if the offer's contingent on anything, such as maintaining a certain GPA. You might also want to follow the employer's fiscal health and other news by setting up a Google alert. Having an offer from a defunct employer isn't worth much.

Moreover, you might want to defer your offer. For example, you might want to consider applying for a judicial clerkship after graduation, or working in another part of the country. So before you accept that offer,[16] you might want to balance the "bird in the hand" with any other options you might have. Think about how risk-averse you are, and act accordingly.

7.2.   If You Haven't Gotten an Offer

There are many reasons why you might not have received an offer. Your employer might not make offers to people who aren't about to graduate; the economy might have shifted downward; or (and this is the bad news) you might not have performed well enough during the summer to have justified getting an offer. You need to figure out why you didn't receive an offer, and you need to find someone who will tell you the truth, if at all possible. Not getting an offer isn't the end of the world, but you need to be prepared to answer questions about what happened. Rehearse your explanation for why you didn't get an offer, so that you don't ramble when you talk about your experience and, if the fault was yours, be prepared to explain how you've changed.

To make the best of a bad situation, you need to find out if it's possible to get a good reference from the employer even though you didn't get an offer. If the reason you didn't get an offer was due to the economy, rather than any fault of yours, you're more likely to be able to get a good reference. Make sure that you ask if

---

[16] NALP has guidelines for accepting and declining offers. *See http://www. nalp.org/fulltextofnalpprinciplesandstandards#Part_V._General_Standards.*

you can get a "good" reference. Asking if you can get a "reference" without the adjective "good" is going to guarantee that all you're likely to get is a "Yep, she worked here" reference—or worse. (Of course, at some law firms, the policy is only to give a "Yep, she worked here" reference whether or not you did a good job—for liability reasons.) If, however, the employer isn't able to give you a good reference, then try to get a debriefing on what you did wrong. Learn from this experience. Everyone makes mistakes. The secret isn't to avoid making mistakes. The secret is to avoid making the same ones over again.

CHAPTER TWELVE.

Evening (Part-Time) Programs/The Nontraditional Law Student

Sure I am this day we are masters of our fate, that the task which has been set before us is not above our strength; that its pangs and toils are not beyond our endurance. As long as we have faith in our own cause and an unconquerable will to win, victory will not be denied us.

—Sir Winston Churchill

Jeff was a nontraditional student; he worked for six years between graduating from high school and attending college. After graduating from college, he went straight to law school.[1] Not only was he older than many first-year law students, but he was also a former Marine and former state trooper. It's fair to say that the Socratic method wasn't intimidating for him. What was intimidating for him, though, was the fairly standard fear of all nontraditional students: Is it possible to return to law school and compete with people who have been students for their entire adult lives?

Many nontraditional students choose to learn law by enrolling in an evening program.[2] We'll discuss issues that nontraditional students face in a day program later on in this chapter.

---

[1] During law school, Jeff worked part-time as a law clerk during both his second and third years, as well as full-time as a law clerk during both summers after his first and second years of law school.

[2] Yes, we know that there are some daytime part-time programs. But we also know that part-time programs aren't very "part-time" at all. They're exhausting. So, out of respect for students who choose to go to law school while working or otherwise taking care of significant responsibilities, we're calling the non-full-time program the "evening" program.

1.   The First Year of the Evening Program

From Jeff's perspective, there is no harder task than trying to go to law school while working full-time. As Nancy has said on several occasions, being a law student in an evening program is like being Ginger Rogers, dancing with Fred Astaire "backwards and in high heels," and making the dance look easy.[3] You'll have to do *almost* everything that the day students do—read cases, prepare for class, synthesize your class notes, outline, draft your writing assignments—and you'll have to do all of that while juggling all of your other responsibilities.

Notice that we used the word "almost." We used this word deliberately. There's not enough time in the day for you to perform all of the possible tasks that the day students might do in law school. To survive (and thrive), you'll have to be efficient. And you'll have to know when to say that enough is enough, close your law books, and get on with the other demands that you're juggling.

Jeff's experience reflects that you can be successful in school if you have a job and a family. He did it. You can, too. But don't be fooled. If you have a family, your life is not going to be easy while you're in law school. You'll be at work all day, and at school most nights until late in the evening. Your weekends will be mostly filled with studying, and there *will* be times that you'll neglect your family. Jeff attended school with several married students who had kids and full-time jobs. Most of these students graduated on time and did very well in school. That does not mean that it was easy on the students or their families. He remains impressed that they were so successful.

Nancy remembers a saying from her law school days. It's possible to have two out of three things simultaneously in law school:

1. Grades.
2. Sleep.
3. A life.

---

[3] According to the official Ginger Rogers Web site, the full quote, attributed to Bob Thaves, is that "[Fred Astaire] was great, but don't forget Ginger Rogers did everything he did backwards . . . and in high heels!" *http://www.gingerrogers.com/about/quotes.html.*

We strongly urge you to fight the temptation to read every possible study guide as a first-year evening student. Because you're not going to have the luxury of time, you might not feel as prepared as you think other first-year students might be. But almost all evening students are in the same boat—they're just as time-pressed as you are, so that race to be more prepared than everyone else is imaginary. Your professors understand that you don't have the same amount of time that the day students have to prepare, and they can take additional time to help you understand tricky points in your week's readings. Our suggestion: Do your readings, listen in class, get together after class (if you have time) to try to figure out what you didn't understand; e-mail your professors to clear up misunderstandings as soon after class as possible; and only if you're still lost should you spend extra time reading nonassigned material. There are still only 24 hours in a day, and you do need to spend some of those hours in non-law-school activities.

1.1. Your Professors and Their Office Hours

As an evening student, most office hours won't work for you. Law school is geared for day students, although many law schools with evening programs will have evening hours for some of the administrative offices. Few law professors, though, will have evening office hours, unless they happen to be night owls.

Most law professors do have fairly flexible schedules, though, and they might be amenable to meeting you for coffee during a weekend. Don't hesitate to ask. Nancy routinely meets with her students (even her day students) on the weekends. She'll meet with students individually, and she'll meet with study groups from time to time.

If you start to feel completely lost in a course, you should make an appointment with the professor who teaches that course and, if your school has an academic support dean, you should make an appointment with that dean as well. Don't wait until the end of the semester in the hope that everything will magically come together at the end of the course.[4] First-year courses are the foundations for

---

[4] Some courses *are* confusing until the very end of the semester. Bankruptcy is one of those courses. But we're talking about first-year courses right now.

every other course in law school. You don't have the luxury of time to let yourself fall behind because you're confused by some significant concept.

1.2. Grades and the Evening Program

Although grades will "count" for you as much as they "count" for the day students, you have something going for you that the day students don't: You have the legitimate argument that you have additional skills that will serve a legal employer exceedingly well. After all, you're going to law school while undertaking at least one additional full-time job. You're working during the day; you're raising children (or helping elderly parents); you're balancing some other 40$^+$-hour per week commitment. *And* you're surviving law school. Add to your time-management ability your ability to work well in teams, your ability to prioritize in a crisis, your ability to delegate, and your ability to maintain a sense of humor, and you can begin to see how your resume can differentiate you from your day-program peers.

By the way, evening students are typically well represented on law reviews, moot court programs, and other prestigious privileges of law school, so don't assume that, as an evening student, you're doomed to getting mediocre grades, either. (And evening students tend to rise through the ranks in practice, as well.)

2.   The Upperclass Curriculum

Evening programs often offer more required upperclass courses than do day programs, on the theory that evening students are more likely to jump into the practice of law after graduation and will need efficient (there's that word again!) guidance as to course selection to help them get started on their legal careers. If your school doesn't require many upper-level courses in your evening program, then we recommend that you take a look at Chapter 10 for course selection advice. And if a course strikes your fancy as just being fun, take it! You get precious little time for fun as an evening student.

3.   Getting the Job Skills That You'll Need

Not only will you need strong reading comprehension skills and strong writing skills, but you'll benefit from finding a way to get some practical skills during law school. Day students typically have the option of taking clinics during the final year of law school and of doing internships. If your law school offers a clinic for evening students, we think that you should move heaven and earth (in other words, take the prerequisite courses) to take advantage of this opportunity, as nothing else in law school provides the "A-ha!" transition from law student to budding lawyer. Internships for people with full-time jobs, though, are well-nigh impossible. You might, however, talk with your employer about shadowing someone in the legal department, or even about spending some time in that department doing intern-like work. Other ways to get experience include becoming a research assistant for a professor (flexible hours!), helping attorneys on pro bono matters, and exploring other options by taking lawyers to lunch for informational interviews. You have to eat; they have to eat. Take 45 minutes to get to know some attorneys and see if they can suggest some ways for you to get some experience while you're going to school. (If your full-time work happens to be law–related, you are one relatively lucky person. You're working your tail off, but your entire day helps you to put what you're learning at night in context.) Finally, don't forget to make an appointment with your career services office. Your career services dean has more experience than you do in helping evening students think about options.

4.   Maintaining Some Semblance of Life Outside Law School

Day program students complain about not having a life. *They have no idea.* But just because they don't know what it's like to do your day job while thinking about what you're going to be covering that night in school (and wondering how few hours of sleep count as "rest"), don't shun the day students. Try to interact with your day program classmates. The connections that you make in law school will help you down the road. Jeff made friends with his evening program classmates because he occasionally took night classes. Virtually all of these classmates were very successful after graduation, and Jeff stays in touch with some of them to this day.

What about your non-law-school friends? Maintaining your outside life is important; if you become totally immersed in law school, you could find yourself without any remaining friends and family. But because we told you, at the beginning of this chapter, that we know that you'll neglect your friends and family from time to time, we know that you're reading this paragraph with a legitimate smirk on your face. The trick is to *neglect them as little as humanly possible.*

You won't be able to go to all of your kid's ball games. But go to some, and not with your Contracts book in front of your face the entire time. If you're going to be with your friends and family, be *with* them—not just present, but there in mind and spirit. When you're studying, if someone wants to crawl into your lap[5] and cuddle, spend a little time cuddling, and then spend some time explaining to him or her what you're reading, and why. (You actually will benefit from explaining what you're learning to someone who's not trained in law. If you can explain law to someone else, then you really understand it.)

You need to retain some semblance of a life, so give yourself permission to be a little unprepared sometimes. Sometimes, someone else will need you more than you'll need to study. Humans outrank words.

5.   Advice for Nontraditional Law Students Going Through the Day Program

Jeff was a nontraditional student when he entered law school, having worked for approximately six years beforehand. He understands what it's like to be older than almost everyone in the classroom, except the professor.[6] Jeff's entering class had some fascinating people who were looking to make a career change.

---

[5] Adult or kid.

[6] Nancy can't resist pointing out that both she and Jeff would now be older than many of the professors, too.

In the class behind Jeff, there were several second- or possibly third-career students. The one that sticks out most for Jeff was a former ACLU activist from Cleveland, Ohio, who was close to 70 years old when he received his JD degree.

Make no mistake; you nontraditional students bring a lot to the table. You have a different perspective from your "straight through school" classmates. You've had to work for a living, so you have ways to measure your accomplishments other than grades on a transcript. When you've actually been in the workforce and then you decide to give up that career to go back to school, you have a dramatically different view of the world from the student who has never really worked in the real world and may not be paying his own tuition.[7] We're not saying that you nontraditional students have a better perspective—just that you tend to have a different one. These differences become evident during various courses.[8]

On average, the main differences between nontraditional and "straight through" students are in the areas of maturity, dedication, and focus. (These differences tend to play out between the evening program students and the "straight through" students as well.) We like "straight through" students a great deal. They have the time and energy to pursue law with an unsurpassed vigor, and their excitement is palpable. We just don't want nontraditional and evening students to feel inferior ever again.

---

[7] Nancy went to college and to law school on what she refers to as a "parent-ship": Her parents paid her tuition, for which she remains eternally grateful.

[8] He noticed the difference in perspective most in Criminal Law and Employment Law.

CHAPTER THIRTEEN

The Judicial Clerkship Process

I have nothing to offer but blood, toil, tears, and sweat.
                                        —Sir Winston Churchill

1.   Should You Clerk?

We think that you should. Both of us had very good experiences when clerking, and we both emerged as stronger writers because of our clerkships. Jeff got his job during an "accidental" interview with his judge; Nancy applied during the traditional clerkship process.

If you really don't think that you can afford (financially or otherwise) to spend one to two years learning at the feet of some-one at the top of his game, and seeing how one of the three branches of government works, then clerking isn't for you. If you are at the beginning of what promises to be a long career, though, then you might want to consider clerking.

2.   Choosing Your List of Judges

You might want to work for a federal appellate judge or a federal district (trial) court judge. You might want to work for a state supreme court judge or state appellate or trial court judge. You might want to work for a magistrate judge or in a specialty court, like the Tax Court or in a bankruptcy court. You can learn a great deal in each of these clerkships. Our advice depends on whether you think you might want to be a trial lawyer or not. If you want to be a trial lawyer, then you might benefit from watching life in a trial court at the federal or state level. Trial court clerkships are extremely busy clerkships, and every day presents its own challenges. Appellate clerkships, often extolled by professors, are in fact a lot like the work that law professors do. They're a more isolated environment and they'll hone your writing skills quite well.

Don't get caught up in the prestige factors of various types of clerkships. Just like the prestige factors of various law schools, you can drive yourself crazy over issues that aren't really within your control. Judges choose *you*, not vice versa.

That being said, our best advice is not to rule yourself out prematurely. Yes, the most obvious candidates are at the top of their classes at the top schools, are the editors in chief of their law reviews, and have discovered cures for all sorts of heretofore incurable diseases. But many judges want to see all manner of people apply for clerkships. Don't rule yourself out from clerkships for which you might actually be qualified, and don't apply to those that are really meant only for a very few special people. Ask some trusted professors and deans (especially your dean of students and career services dean) for advice.[1]

3.   Your Application Packet

Check with your career services office to see if the judges in whom you're interested participate in OSCAR,[2] which has its own process for recommendation letters, and to see in what time frame those judges want your application. To be safe, you'll want three letters of recommendation (at least two of which should come from faculty members who can talk about your research and writing skills and your work ethic—and about how well you work as part of a team) and a good writing sample. If you happen to know a judge, or know someone who knows that judge, and that person can write you a *good* recommendation letter, then definitely add that person to your list of recommenders.

---

[1] You can get a good list of judges from your career services office and from Westlaw and LEXIS.

[2] OSCAR stands for the Online System for Clerkship Application and Review. *See https://oscar.uscourts.gov.*

When we say "good" recommendation, we're serious. Ask your potential recommenders if they can write you a good recommendation. Don't just ask people who know you a little bit; ask people who know you well and can say, with some specificity, why you are a very good candidate for a clerkship. If the person you've asked for a recommendation hesitates, even a little bit, in saying yes, find someone else. A lukewarm recommendation is a kiss of death.

Your cover letter should lead with your strengths in the first paragraph. If you're at the top of your class, on law review, or a top moot court competitor, say so—in that first paragraph. You want to make sure that whoever's screening the application reads beyond that paragraph. If you don't have the traditional law review, top grades, and other bells and whistles to put in your first paragraph, put in something else that makes you stand out. Some judges get hundreds of applications, and the screeners can spend fewer than two minutes per application deciding which applications to read in detail. Obviously, your cover letter should be free of typographical errors and should be formal—in other words, not as breezily written as this survival manual.

Don't forget to tailor your writing sample to the type of clerkship for which you're applying. If you're applying for a trial court clerkship, look for a sample that analyzes some issue that a trial court would want to see, such as a rule of evidence; if you're applying for an appellate court, consider a sample that would interest an appellate court, such as one discussing a split in the circuits.

4.   The Only Two Acceptable Answers to a Clerkship Offer

There are only two acceptable answers to an offer: "Yes, Your Honor, I'd be delighted to clerk for you," or "Your Honor, I'd love to, but I just accepted a clerkship offer yesterday."

Why are these the only two acceptable answers? First, you shouldn't apply to any judge for whom you wouldn't want to clerk. Don't waste that judge's time. Second, once you have accepted a clerkship offer, don't waste any other judge's time, either: Withdraw any pending applications. Do not, under any circumstances, accept a judge's clerkship offer and then renege to take another offer from a different judge or from another employer. Judges have notoriously long memories, and given the amount of discretion that they wield, they aren't to be trifled with—not to mention that when you renege on a judge's offer, you've not only irritated that judge on your *own* behalf, you've now irritated the judge on *your school's* behalf. It'll be a while before that judge considers choosing another clerk from your school, given your lack of manners.

5.   Before You Start Your Clerkship

You should find out if there are particular courses that your judge wants you to take. Nancy's judge wanted her to take Federal Jurisdiction, so she did. If there are other things that your judge wants you to do to prepare for the clerkship, then do them.

Some judges will let you accept a post-clerkship job before you begin your clerkship, as long as you recuse yourself from working on any matters involving your post-clerkship employer. Other judges prefer that you not make any post-clerkship plans until a few months before your clerkship will end. Clarifying this matter— as well as clarifying the issue of whether your judge will let you take time off to study for a bar exam[3]—before you start will avoid any awkwardness.

6.   What Judges Value

Judges value:

- Good analytic skills.
- Good research skills.
- Good writing skills.

---

[3] Nancy took the California Bar Exam the February after her clerkship ended; one of her co-clerks took a bar exam before his clerkship began, and his subsequent admission to the bar enabled him to get a bump in pay during his clerkship year.

- Accuracy, speed, and honesty (telling them if you think that they're wrong).
- Help in drafting opinions that don't get reversed.

Judges detest:

- Sloth.
- Gossip.
- Abuse of others inside or outside the chambers.
- Lack of discretion or a breach of confidentiality.

Clerking for a judge is a privilege and an honor. Enjoy your time in this very special job.

CHAPTER FOURTEEN

The Bar Exam

*There are no secrets to success. It is the result of preparation, hard work,
[and] learning from failure.*

—Gen. Colin Powell

Although the bar examination is likely to be one of the hardest
tests, if not the hardest test, you'll ever take, it need not be a debil-
itating experience. Jeff has had the "opportunity" to take three
different bar examinations[1] and has been successful each time
(Ohio in 1987, Texas in 2004, and Nevada in 2008). (Nancy has
taken two:[2] California in 1987 and Nevada in 2007, also successful
both times.) Jeff was also a bar examiner in Ohio—the one who
wrote the commercial law questions.[3] He can honestly say that the
Texas bar exam (2004) seemed more difficult than the Ohio exam
(1987), and that the Nevada Bar exam (2008) was the hardest test
that he has ever taken. Part of the difficulty inherent in the Texas
and Nevada exams was due to the amount of time that had passed
between graduating from law school and sitting for those two
exams.

There is simply no substitute for leaving one intense educational experience and entering another one almost immediately.
For many of you, studying for the bar will be far more intense than
your experience of studying in law school. For Jeff, the stress of bar
preparation came not from a fear of failing the bar but from a
recognition that no one with his class rank had ever failed the bar
before. Understandably, he did not want to be the first. It's amazing
what drives people to do well: Sometimes it's the desire to do well,
and sometimes it's the fear of failure. As Nancy often says, right
before she's about to miss a deadline: "Fear is a great motivator."

---

[1] He waived into Nebraska.

[2] She waived into Ohio, Nebraska, and Texas.

[3] In an illustration of one of life's little ironies, Nancy swore that she would
never date (1) a bar examiner, (2) a lawyer, (3) someone who was allergic to cats, or

It is safe to say that the most "law" that you'll ever know is the amount of law that you have in your brain on the first day of the bar exam.[4] It's also *very* safe to say that the exact minute that you walk out of the room on the last day of the bar exam, you'll start forgetting everything that you don't use regularly in your practice.[5]

We strongly recommend that you take studying for the bar seriously. These exams are given, at most, twice a year. Some states place caps on how many times you can take their bar exams. You do not want to get all of the way through law school and then not pass the bar. And, if at all possible, you want to pass the bar on the first try. Statistically speaking, failing the exam on your first try can have very bad long-term consequences for you. Some employers will withdraw their offers of employment. Moreover, at least back when Jeff was a bar examiner, the chances of passing the examination on the second try drop to only about 50/50, and down to one chance in three for the third and subsequent exams.

1.   Approaches to Studying for the Exam

Bar exam preparation, like the exam itself, is a marathon, not a sprint. Give it the respect that it is due. Simply stated, the hare rarely wins this race; there is just too much to learn and too little time within which to do it (especially if you chose to take very few "bar courses" during law school). Even if you took most of the bar courses in school, there is a lot of material to rehash. And if you went to a national law school, you likely didn't cover anything related to a specific state. Most states will ask questions about their own law during their exams. For more information about a particular state's bar exam, you should check out *http://www.ncbex.org*.

---

(4) someone of the opposite political party. And, of course, now she's married to someone who's all four of those.

[4] At least until you walk into your next bar exam.

[5] Nancy has one caveat: There will be one totally useless bit of information that you just can't get out of your mind, even 20 or more years later. For her, it's California Probate Code §240 (intestate succession). She is convinced that Probate Code §240 has pushed some perfectly useful things out of her brain. She wants those things back. Now.

In general, we believe that you should use the same study methods for the bar examination that you used during law school. If you are a study group type of person, use a study group to get ready for the bar. If you are a go-it-alone person, then go it alone. If you were a blend of the two, as Jeff was, then use that method. If you were successful with your particular approach in law school, why would you want to abandon that approach now? (On the other hand, if you weren't so successful in law school, now's a good time to search your soul to figure out what worked well and what didn't.)

Especially now, do not let peer pressure force you into a different study method from the one that you know and trust. Some people get absolutely crazy when preparing for the bar exam; do not let their craziness throw you off your game. Remember, your professional life is at stake.

1.1. Old Exams

Ohio, Texas, and Nevada all publish prior bar exam questions, as do many other states. As with our earlier recommendation, we strongly suggest that you look at prior exam questions when studying for your bar exam. There is no better method of gleaning the bar examiners' thinking and question presentation methodology than reviewing the examiners' old exams.

Some states will not only release their old exams, but also "best answers" to go with the individual exams. These answers are golden, as they tell you what the examiners in that state believe to be most critical in answering the particular questions. When reviewing the questions, look at how the answers are organized. The bar examiners are giving you a road map for how they want your response to look when they give you the best answers. Hint: Give them what they want. We know this advice sounds basic, but just like law school, your chances of doing well go up considerably if you give the examiners what they want as far as answer structure and organization go.

1.2. Setting the Odds

Some states, like Nevada, offer a list of "potential" exam topics, many of which will appear on the exam and some of which won't.

If you are like Jeff, you'll sit down and look at the overall history (e.g., the past ten years) as well as the recent history (the past five years) and come up with a chart to determine what the odds are that any particular exam topic will appear as an essay question on your particular bar examination. (Nancy just left everything to chance.) In some cases, you are virtually guaranteed to have certain subjects, like Contracts or Constitutional Law—the only issue is how many questions on these topics will appear on the test. Obviously, you want to spend time on all of the possible subjects, as you might be asked a question on the exam about that particular topic, even though the topic appeared in several recent examinations. What we are discussing here is focusing your study on several topics that will have a larger overall effect on your passing the exam, rather than treating all topics equally.

Other states will tell you how many questions that you will have on each subject, so there is no ambiguity on that issue. The issue then becomes, as between the various topic areas, on which ones should you spend the most time studying? Here is a simple answer to that question: Multistate Bar Examination (MBE) topics carry more weight than non-MBE topics. Why is that? Because almost all of the MBE topics will also be appearing on the essay portion of the examination, you'll need to know these topics extremely well. More important, you'll need to know the differences between the "national" view and the "state" view on the MBE subjects.

We disagree about how to allocate time for studying. Nancy believes in divvying time equally among all subjects and then, only during the last two weeks before the bar, focusing on the areas that are the weakest for her. Jeff, on the other hand, believes that you can objectively determine which subjects are most important (by percentage contribution to your total score on the exam) to passing the exam and focusing on them, while still studying the other subject areas. Jeff never stopped studying some subjects for his recent Nevada Bar experience; he simply reduced the amount of time spent on those subjects. Others might give you a different philosophy. But let there be no mistake: Don't skip any subject entirely. There are certain truths in life. Toast falls butter-side down. Just as you need to get off the couch, your cat will jump into your lap, flop onto her back with that "scratch-me-on-the-belly" look on her face, and start to purr. And if you skip studying a subject altogether, that subject is guaranteed to be a question when you sit for the exam.

1.3. The MPRE

Not only will most states require the "regular" bar exam, but you'll likely have to take the Multistate Professional Responsibility Exam (MPRE) as well. You can get information on the MPRE at *http://www.ncbex.org/multistate-tests/mpre/*. We've each taken the MPRE three times, not because we've failed it, but because our scores were "stale" given the length of time between some of our bar exams. Imagine our joy. At least it's only a morning-long exam.

1.4. Bar Review Courses and Other Study Aids

We have taken five bar exams between the two of us (so far) and, each time, we took a bar review course to help us review the topics on which the bar examiners were going to test us. If you can at all afford to take a bar review course, we wholeheartedly recommend that you take one. Sure, you could go back through all of your law school notes, go to the library, buy old bar review books from eBay, and probably muddle through, but your stress level will be sky-high. You'll snap like a twig.

If you're not particularly good at multiple-choice exams, and Nancy is one of those people who is horrible at them, there is one book that she particularly recommends: Kimm Alayne Walton & Steve Emanuel, *Strategies & Tactics for the MBE Multistate Bar Exam: Multistate Bar Exam* (Aspen, 2010). (Although Aspen is also our publisher, and Nancy lectures for Emanuel Bar Review—and she worked a little bit on the newest edition of the Walton and Emanuel book—all of those relationships occurred after she used this book to study for the Nevada Bar.) This book helped her understand how to read the questions in the MBE, how to sift through common tricks on the MBE, and how to study for the MBE efficiently.

About a month before the Nevada Bar, which Nancy took in July 2007, she went through the traditional panic and bought every study aid being sold on eBay. She even used some of them. We have come to a unified conclusion: At some point while studying for the bar, you *will* panic. Inside your head, that panic will sound something like this: "There isn't enough time to get ready; I can't possibly learn all this stuff; I'm going to fail for *sure*." You'll get flashbacks to your first semester of law school and that awful feeling of being woefully unprepared. Don't worry (too much). It's normal. You need to find a way to get past that panic and continue with your work: preparing for the bar exam.

2.   Working While Studying for the Exam

Your life will be much less stressful if you don't work while you're studying for the bar exam. Unfortunately, working is a requirement for lots of folks sitting for the bar examination. Even if you work, unless you and your family will be in dire straits, you really should take off the last two weeks before the bar to focus on the final memorization process. Four weeks off is better. Not working for at least six weeks is best.

If you must work while you're studying, then you'll need to start studying earlier and be more organized in your approach to the exam. Even if you are taking a bar review course, you can—and should—begin your own preparation before the bar review class begins.

Most study classes are based on about a 12-week schedule (counting the 4 to 6 weeks of class, plus the equivalent in postlecture study time). In contrast, you've known that you are going to be taking the bar exam for three years (or four years, if you're in evening school). There is no legitimate reason to delay some preliminary work on the exam, especially if you're working full-time before the exam. Take a look at the topics that will appear on the exam. (You'll find these on the Web site of the bar association of the state giving the bar exam.) Go find those outlines that you prepared in law school, sift through the stack, and find some that correspond with the bar exam topics. You can begin to review them while waiting for the bar review class to begin.

Our single most important bit of advice while you take the bar review class is this: *Memorize early and often.* Your brain can take only so much in at once. By the time that you're only two weeks from the exam start date, your brain will rebel if you try to cram 12 different subjects' worth of memorization in. In an ideal world, you'd start memorizing a subject immediately after the end of that subject's bar review lecture. Make flash cards. Make tapes and listen to them while working out. Count elements of causes of action, instead of sheep, while you're drifting off to sleep. But memorize *early*.

3.   How Long to Study Each Day

Returning to our mantra about bar preparation being a marathon, not a sprint, here's one cautionary note: Spending too much time too early on studying will likely result in burnout and losing your "edge" when you need it most (when you walk into the exam for the first day). For his first bar exam, Jeff felt almost perfectly prepared. He felt that if he had had just two or three more days, he actually would have been perfectly prepared. That feeling is exactly where you want to be when you walk in the door. Your knowledge base is not "full"; you're not burned out; you're sharp. On the other end of the continuum would be a person who has burned the candle at both ends, who shows up for the exam totally cooked and looking like he needs a serious vacation. Such a person would be so sleep-deprived that he has already hurt his chances of passing the exam.

From Jeff's view, you can likely get by with studying in total somewhere between eight to ten hours a day, *on average* during the preparation period. (Nancy thinks that you can get by with six to eight hours a day, on average.) But what we mean by an hour of studying is, well, an hour (60 minutes) of studying, not putting in 35 to 40 minutes of every hour "studying" and then walking around the library chatting with your friends. That is not an *hour* of studying.[6] Jeff's suggestion of an average means that you start a bit lighter on the study time and then slowly ramp it up as the number of subjects increases and the exam is getting closer. Then, as in training for any sport, the study and preparation time tapers just before the exam so that you can go in fresh and well rested. Treat studying for the bar as you would treat any other full-time job.

Jeff built into his preparation schedule some time for working out, just as he had in law school. He called that time his "brain break."

---

[6] And when you're a lawyer, that's not an hour of billable time, either.

(Your brain break might involve video games, napping, playing with kids or pets, or other fun activities.) When he resumed his studies later in the day, he almost always felt refreshed and ready to go again.

If you start off putting in 12-hour study days and then increase from that number, we believe that you are nearly guaranteed to burn out before the exam. Once you've lost the edge,[7] it's almost impossible to get it back. The reason for having a game plan going into the exam is to increase your chances of passing the exam.

4.   The Exam Itself

Most states now give takers a choice of writing or using a computer to take the exam. If you're using a computer, this hint is not relevant. But if you're writing your exam—as in using a pen and paper—you simply *must* write legibly. *If the examiner cannot read your written response, you will flunk the exam.* As a former bar examiner in Ohio, Jeff has numerous stories about horrible handwriting. No examiner is going to take the time to parse through your writing to figure out what you're trying to say. Examiners, and in some states, exam graders, have too many tests to grade to spend any time at all trying to decipher your hieroglyphics. Jeff's favorite example of a disastrous answer was one that looked very much like an EKG strip: horizontal lines with periodic vertical lines extending above and below the horizontal lines. "EKG Man" didn't pass.[8]

---

[7] Losing the edge, like losing "that loving feeling," is not a good thing. *See Top Gun* (Paramount Pictures 1986); *see also http://www.imdb.com/title/tt0092099/quotes* (referring to losing that loving feeling). Nancy watched *Top Gun* once a week, every week, for six weeks while studying for the California Bar Exam. (In a movie theatre, back before videotapes were common or DVDs even existed.) *Top Gun* was her theme movie for that bar exam.

[8] In Ohio, the bar examiners gathered before and after the examination to discuss questions and a variety of other topics. Generally, they also asked about responses that they had received to see if anyone else had received something similar. The "EKG strip" writer was a topic of discussion after the bar examination, as no one was able to understand what "EKG Man" had written. That person did not pass the bar exam, regardless of what or how much law he or she knew.

In terms of your environment, you might want to scope out the physical layout before the first day of the bar exam. Most bar exams are given in cavernous rooms and can be fairly noisy. If you work best in silence, get a set of earplugs.

We talked earlier about how to answer law school essay exams. You should use some variant of IRAC. Well, for the essay portions of the bar exam, you should use that same approach. The bar exam is not about just knowing the correct answer to the questions. For example, the call of the question might well be "Is there a contract? Explain." Simply writing "yes" won't give you a passing grade on that question. From a bar examiner's perspective, you could very well have simply tossed a mental coin to reach your conclusion that "yes" was the correct answer. You need to explain why you think that there is a contract. Your explanation will show that you understand the appropriate legal concepts. In a sense, your explanation of why you concluded that there is a contract is what determines whether you've written a passing answer or not. *Essay exams are much more about your ability to explain how you got to the correct answer* than they are about the legal conclusion.

You might be surprised (even relieved) to know that numerous people have been known to pass a bar exam essay even if they reach some incorrect conclusions on questions. Let's revisit the call of our hypothetical question ("Is there a contract? Explain.") Even if you reached the wrong conclusion, but you were able to identify the proper elements involved, to identify the appropriate facts to analyze, and did a thorough analysis, the fact that you reached the wrong conclusion didn't get in the way of demonstrating that you knew the law.

4.1. Sleep

It goes without saying but we'll say it anyway: You should have front-loaded your studying for the bar exam, so that there's no need for an all-nighter study session the day before the exam starts. As best you can (we understand that pre-bar-exam jitters can make sleep a bit difficult), you need to get a good night's sleep before the bar. As a matter of fact, try not to study that last afternoon and evening before the bar. Play golf. Go to a movie. Do something that relieves stress. It's perfectly okay to look over your study materials during the nights of the actual bar exam, but don't obsess. At this point, you're not going to cram any more information into your brain. Looking over that information gives you something to do rather than "stress out" over what did or didn't occur during that day's exam.

4.2. *Eating*

You've got to eat lunch, so what are you going to do about it? Many folks go out to eat. We weren't "go out to eat with the gang" folks. We didn't want to leave anything to chance, especially a car accident or traffic jam that would have had us returning to the exam late, and being locked out from the afternoon session. For his Nevada exam, Jeff didn't have any study partners, so he took his lunch in a cooler and ate in his car. That way, he had some quiet time, and he couldn't really hear anyone talking about the exam.[9] For his Ohio exam (his first exam right after law school), Jeff ate lunch with his study partners, all of whom brought their lunches. They had agreed that they would *not* talk about the exam during lunch. They didn't, and he went back into the exam refreshed every day. One last piece of food advice: Try to eat a light lunch. You don't want something heavy sitting in your stomach, doing its best to put you to sleep during the early afternoon session of the exam. (Nor do you want to eat something that might give you food poisoning. Watch out for things that could spoil.) You need to be sharp for all sessions; your diet can make a difference.

5.   Daily Postexam Session Aftermath

Lots of your classmates will gather every night of the bar to rehash what they saw, and the topics that they think were covered. Don't join in! It's not helpful, and it could be flat-out wrong.

---

[9] During her California exam, Nancy and her best friend packed their lunches and then took a long walk each day. For the Nevada exam, Jeff brought Nancy lunch and then hung out with her while she played video poker. We live in Las Vegas, and that particular exam was given directly across the street from a local casino. Jeff's Nevada bar exam was given in the conference room of another casino.

For example, a question could have been about either Constitutional Law or Evidence. If you thought it was about one and everyone else thought it was about the other, do you really want to have a detailed and possibly heated discussion about it? Even if your friends are correct, is there anything that you can do about your mistake now? Nope. So let it go.[10]

During the bar exam, you need to develop a type of selective amnesia. We mean that you need to be able to jot down your list of topics that you think were covered, so that you can reevaluate what's left to be tested. Then you need to let go of the portion of the test that's now finished. You can't change what you wrote so far, so fretting about it will do you no good at all. This is very much like golf,[11] where you need to forget your last bad shot and focus on the shot in front of you. There is plenty to time to rehash this information when the bar exam is all over (although, of course, we recommend against that, too).

---

[10] When Jeff was taking the Ohio bar, one of the bar review courses had a practice of telling its students what topics had been covered that day (as told to them by various students that they trusted). It turns out the students were wrong on one topic, claiming that it was an Evidence question, when it was really a Constitutional Law question. In any event, it made a difference; some people used that information and then allocated their time to review materials for the next day, avoiding one topic and reviewing the other. There was more than a bit of turmoil the next night when grumbles were heard up and down the library aisles about studying X instead of studying Y. Do yourself a favor and use your own judgment about what has been covered. If you don't trust your memory, make a list at lunch and then again when you leave for the day.

[11] Or any other sport, including but not limited to ballroom dancing.

_____

CHAPTER FIFTEEN

A Few Last Survival Tips

Beware that, when fighting monsters, you yourself do not become a monster . . . for when you gaze long into the abyss, the abyss gazes also into you.

—Friedrich Nietzsche

A true leader has the confidence to stand alone, the courage to make tough decisions, and the compassion to listen to the needs of others. He does not set out to be a leader, but becomes one by the equality of his actions and the integrity of his intent.

—Gen. Douglas MacArthur

Okay, we're about to send you off into the world of law school and beyond, armed with this survival manual and with the hope that you will not just survive but thrive. As we were writing this book, we had some random thoughts that didn't quite fit in anywhere else, so we're putting them here.

According to one of Nancy's colleagues, Dean Frank Durand, remember that it's easy to have a bad time in law school. Having a good time requires proactivity. Take charge of your time in law school. Revel in the challenge. It's a new experience. Throw yourself into that experience wholeheartedly.

Whenever you get frustrated in law school (and you will), whenever you can't remember why you chose to get a law degree, whenever you think that any other path would be better than staying in school, remember this: Going to law school requires a vision of why you want to get the degree. Maybe you want to be a lawyer. Maybe you want the knowledge for its own sake, and you never plan to practice law. Maybe you wanted to stay in school, and law school seemed more interesting than other choices. Whatever your reason, at one point, you had a vision for why you chose law school.[1]

_____

[1] If you never had a vision for why you chose law school, then you might have a different problem. As Lewis Carroll said, "If you don't know where you are going, any road will get you there."

During your most difficult moments, go back to that vision. Ask yourself if it still rings true. If it doesn't, then it's time to take stock and ask yourself if your vision of surviving law school makes sense.

If, however, your vision of surviving law school does ring true, then spend a little time walking yourself through the steps that you'll need to take to get from where you are now to that day when you walk across the stage at graduation. And when you make it to graduation day, know that we're there with you in spirit, cheering you on.

Jeff's First-Year Schedule

	Mon	Tues	Wed	Thurs	Fri	Sat	Sun
6:00	Prep for Contracts	Prep for Torts	Prep for Contracts	Prep for Torts	Prep for Contracts		
6:30							
7:00						Prep for study group	Prep for study group
7:30							
8:00	Contracts	Torts	Contracts	Torts	Contracts		
8:30							
9:00	Prep Real Property		Prep Real Property		Prep Real Property	Study group	Study group
9:30							
10:00	Real Property	Legal Writing	Real Property	Legal Writing	Real Property		
10:30							
11:00		Legal Writing assignments		Legal Writing assignments			
11:30	Work out/ physical training		Work out/ physical training		Work out/ physical training		
12:00							
12:30							

1:00						Study group
1:30						Study group
2:00	Outline/ study		Outline/ study		Outline/ study	
2:30						
3:00	Outline/ study/ study group	Outline/ study group	Outline/ study/ study group	Outline/ study group	Outline/ study/ study group	Work out/ physical training
3:30						
4:00						
4:30						
5:00						
5:30	Study Group/ Outline		Study Group/ Outline		Study Group/ Outline	
6:00						
6:30						
7:00						
7:30						

Nancy's First-Year Schedule

Week 1	Week 2	Week 3	Week N
Review Week 1 Contracts	Review Week 1 Contracts; add Week 2 Contracts; condense material; put Week 1 & Week 2 notes away for good	Review condensed Week 1 & Week 2 material; add Week 3 Contracts material; condense all material; add discarded Week 3 notes to discarded Week 1 & Week 2 notes	Review condensed material from prior weeks; add Week N Contracts material; condense all material; add discarded Week N notes to all discarded prior weeks' notes
Review Week 1 Torts	Review Week 1 Torts; add Week 2 Torts; condense material; put Week 1 & Week 2 notes away for good	Review condensed Week 1 & Week 2 material; add Week 3 Torts material; condense all material; add discarded Week 3 notes to discarded Week 1 & Week 2 notes	Review condensed material from prior weeks; add Week N Torts material; condense all material; add discarded Week N notes to all discarded prior weeks' notes

Week 1	Week 2	Week 3	Week N
Review Week 1 Civ Pro[1]	Review Week 1 Civ Pro; add Week 2 Civ Pro; condense material; put Week 1 & Week 2 notes away for good	Review condensed Week 1 & Week 2 material; add Week 3 Civ Pro material; condense all material; add discarded Week 3 notes to discarded Week 1 & Week 2 notes	Review condensed material from prior weeks; add Week N Civ Pro material; condense all material; add discarded Week N notes to all discarded prior weeks' notes

---

[1] That's Civil Procedure in "law school speak."

Jeff's Upperclass Schedule

	Mon	Tues	Wed	Thurs	Fri	Sat	Sun
6:00	Work out		Work out		Work out	Work out	
6:30							
7:00	Prep Negot Instrument		Prep Negot Instrument		Prep Negot Instrument		
7:30		Prep Bankruptcy		Prep Bankruptcy			
8:00	Negot Instrument	Bankruptcy	Negot Instrument	Bankruptcy	Negot Instrument		
8:30							
9:00	Prep Land Use		Prep Land Use		Prep Land Use	Outline/ Prep for study group	Outline/ Prep for study group
9:30							
10:00	Land Use	outline	Land Use	outline	Land Use		
10:30							
11:00	outline		outline		outline		
11:30							
12:00	Clerk with law firm	Prep Ad Law	Clerk with law firm	Prep Ad Law	Clerk with law firm	Study group	
12:30							

1:00		Admin Law		Admin Law			
1:30							
2:00							
2:30							
3:00							
3:30							
4:00	Law Review/moot ct	Outline/study/prep for study group	Law Review/moot ct	Outline/study/prep for study group	Law Review/moot ct		
4:30							
5:00							
5:30							
6:00	Study group	Law Review/moot ct	Study group	Law Review/moot ct	Study group		
6:30							
7:00							
7:30							
8:00							

Ode to a Hypothetical: The Saga of Dan and Vic as Nancy's Twisted Brain Might Think About It[1]

Here is the way that Nancy's mental script might have approached the hypothetical, as she read it, phrase by phrase. Any resemblance to an actual mental script is purely coincidental.

Component of Hypothetical	Nancy's Mental Script While Reading That Component
One night,	I'll bet that "night" has something to do with this question. Hey! Doesn't burglary have a "night" component?
when it was raining lightly,	"Rain" has to be in there for some reason. Does burglary have a "rain" component? I don't remember one. Did we read cases that distinguished "rain" from "nonrain" situations? Maybe the rain has no effect either way and it's in here merely to distract me from answering the real question (a "red herring").
Dan went looking for Vic,	Where do these names come from anyway? "Dan." "Vic." Couldn't they come up with names that were a little more interesting? I'll abbreviate the names in my answer (they're too long to write). I'll use D for "Dan" and V for "Vic." Cool: D also stands for Defendant,

---

[1] Nancy first wrote a version of this stream-of-consciousness illustration in 1999.

Component of Hypothetical	Nancy's Mental Script While Reading That Component
	which is—I guess—what Dan is, and V stands for Victim.
saying "I'll get that guy for cheating me out of $100."	D sure seems mad at V. Is it an excuse to a charge of burglary if D is just retaliating for something V did? What does the phrase "I'll get that guy" mean, anyway? I'll "get" him in court? I'll "get" him in the parking lot?
Dan took a loaded pistol with him.	It sure *looks* as if D has some violence on his mind. Why else would he have a loaded pistol? On the other hand, maybe he has another reason for carrying a pistol. He could be a police officer or a detective. If there's no other reason that makes sense, though, this starts to look as if D is planning something that bodes ill for V.
Not knowing where Vic lived,	Well, maybe D *isn't* trying to harm V. After all, he's not looking up V's address, etc.
Dan wandered around the city for several hours.	Why? Is Dan casing the neighborhood? Trying to calm down? The darn hypothetical doesn't *say* why! Can I make a reasonable inference? **Note to me:** Any inference needs to explain what facts in the hypothetical I used to make the inference. *Must use facts.*
Suddenly,	Is "suddenly" here for a reason? Does rain ever start *"not suddenly"*? Or is this just a segue into the next set of important facts?
it began to rain heavily.	There's that rain thing again. Why is "rain" so darn important?
Dan smashed	"Smashing" = "breaking," doesn't it?

Component of Hypothetical	Nancy's Mental Script While Reading That Component
a window in the very first house he saw	"Very first house" doesn't seem to be a planned act. Maybe D's just trying to get in out of the rain. *Wait a minute:* Who breaks into houses to get out of the rain? That *can't* be normal.
and entered.	Well, there's the "entering" component of burglary. At least *that'll* be easy to prove in my answer.
He remained inside the house	What's he doing inside the house? Sitting around? Developing an "intent"?
until the rain stopped.	This makes it look as if D's only intent is to get out of the rain. I wonder how long he stayed inside. He's already walked around for several hours. Did he enter at night, or was it already morning when he entered? Did he leave to walk around while it was still night? What happens if he entered at night but left in the morning? Does the "night" element of burglary mean that all of his "burglary" activities have to fit within the "night" requirement, or can he start at night and end in the morning (or midday, for that matter)?
As Dan was about to leave,	Has he committed a felony yet? Has he *intended* to commit one? If he's leaving without the intent to commit a felony, maybe he can't be charged with burglary.
Vic came in the front door.	Well, I'll bet that *Dan* was surprised!
Startled,	Would Dan be any less startled if someone else besides Vic entered the house? Is Dan

Component of Hypothetical	Nancy's Mental Script While Reading That Component
	startled because it's Vic, or because Dan's inside someone's house and didn't expect anyone else to be there?
Dan pulled out his gun	Did Dan plan to shoot Vic? He carried a gun on purpose, but the hypo said that he didn't know whose house it was when he broke in, so he can't have "planned" to shoot Vic *in the house*. I guess we can rule out "attempted murder of Vic" as the felony that he might have had in mind. He might have had that felony in mind while he was walking around outside, but he didn't have that particular felony in mind while he was inside the Home of the Unnamed Owner.
and fired one shot,	In which direction? Was Dan *aiming* at Vic? Did the gun go off on purpose or because Dan was startled?
missing Vic.	I'm sure glad that Dan wasn't charged with attempted murder or attempted assault, or I'd have to discuss *that* in my answer, too. Should I mention it just in passing?
Dan then ran out the door.	Why did Dan run? To get away from Vic? Because he's ashamed that he's a bad shot? Because he reacted quickly to being startled? Does he even know that it's Vic that he shot at? *(Note that the rules of grammar are being flung to the wind while thinking about exams.)*
As it turned out,	Big surprise here—*not*. Law professors must have a twisted sense of humor. *Sadists*.
Dan had broken into Vic's house;	This sort of thing only seems to happen in law exam hypotheticals. As Larry "Bubbles" Brown says, "Coincidence? Perhaps. . . ."

Component of Hypothetical	Nancy's Mental Script While Reading That Component
	See http://en.wikipedia.org/wiki/Larry_Bubbles_ Brown.
Dan did not know whose house it was when he broke in.	Does burglary require that the criminal know who owns the house (um, I mean, the "dwelling")?
Dan has been charged with burglary.	I'll bet I need to recite the elements of burglary in my answer. What are they again? (1) the breaking and entering (2) of a dwelling (3) of another (4) in the nighttime (5) with intent to commit a felony (6) therein. I'd better make sure that my answer addresses all six of those elements.
What result?	I'd better organize my answer. There's a lot of stuff here for me to discuss.

INDEX